THIS BOOK BELONGS TO

_____

_____

DATE

_____

Prince Coloring Book: A Tribute to His Musical Genius
Copyright © 2018 Andre Hollingsworth

Illustrated by Andre Hollingsworth
Edited by Menia Buckner

ISBN-13: 978-1986703567

If you are using a marker please place a blank piece of paper behind the coloring pages to prevent bleed-though.

Connect with Andre Hollingsworth online at:

 Art_by_andre

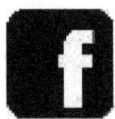 Art by Andre Hollingsworth

For information about custom editions or corporate purchases, please contact Andre at artbyandremn@gmail.com.

A portion of the proceeds of this book will support Connections to Independence (C2i) in Minneapolis Minnesota. The Mission of C2i is to provide unique programming and advocacy for foster care youth, ages 15-24, to promote a successful and healthy transition to living independently as they reach adulthood.
www.c2iyouth.org

Made in the USA

Prince

Icon (EYE-kahn): a graphic representation of something; a person or thing that is symbolic or is a noted figure.

Who would break all the rules that sought to define him outside of how he would define himself? Who would create a genre of music and a look, setting a tone that would revolutionize the face of music? Who would defy a music label and change his name to prove a point, thereby setting a precedent for reclaiming one's creativity? Who would have a love for his hometown and insist on remaining connected to it by establishing his base there and constantly giving back? Who would usurp the color purple and cause the whole world to pay homage by lighting their buildings and bridges in purple upon his untimely demise?

The multitalented musician/singer/fashion guru/philanthropist:

"His Royal Highness" Prince Rogers Nelson.

– Menia Buckner

Hoop Dreams

"On my little basketball team, when we needed to kill something, we'd give the ball to Prince. He could dribble like crazy. He's a real good athlete. He just didn't have the size that some of those other kids did, but he was quick, and he was really smart. He didn't have to study too hard to do junior high work; he'd do it once, and he had it. I always said, 'Make sure you put your education before music,' and he was like, 'Yeah, sure.'"
Gene Anderson, 1971 Bryant Junior High basketball head coach/Southwest Journal March 10, 2015

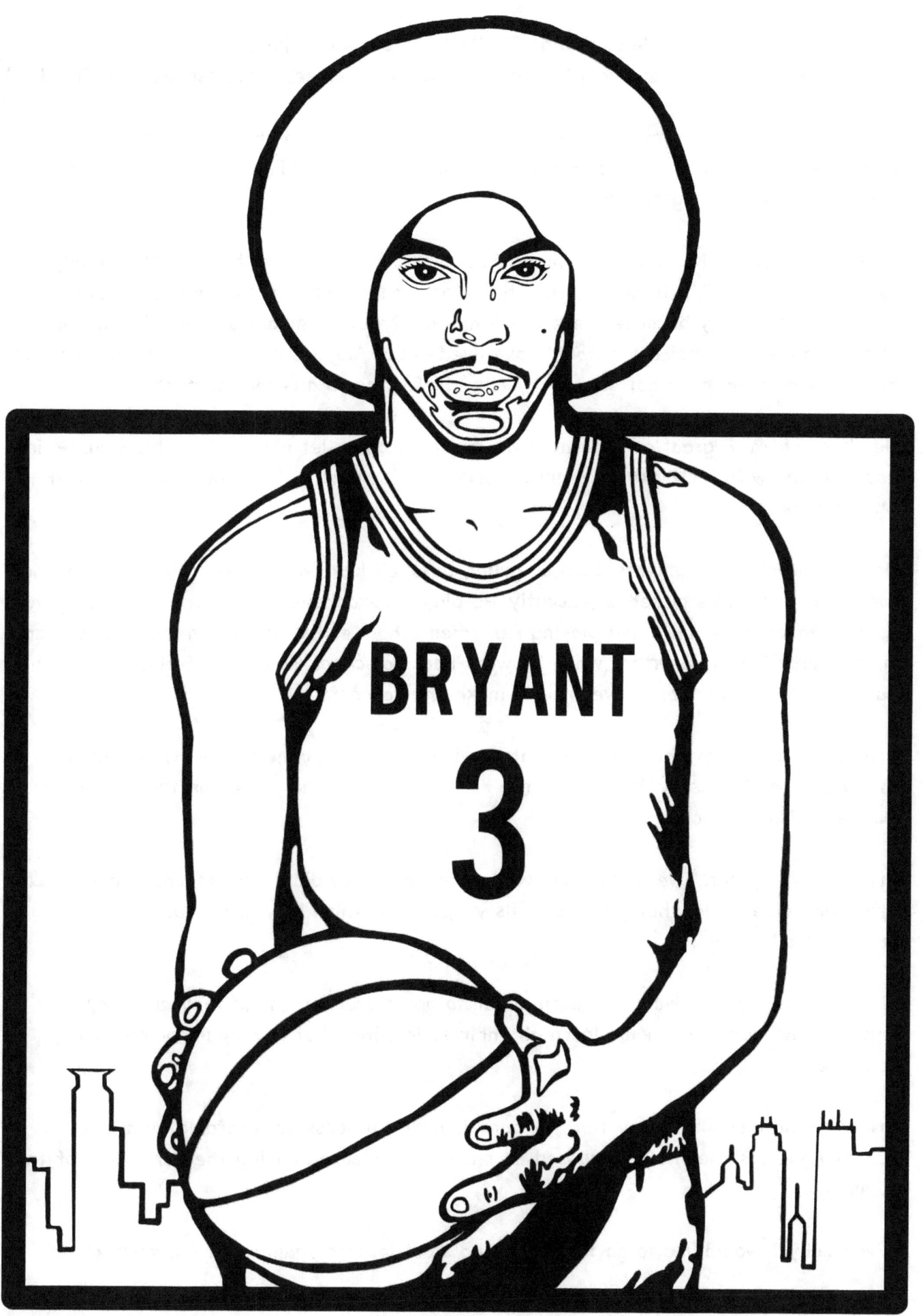

Nelson Finds It 'Hard to Become Known'

Prince's first interview at age 17 in the Central High Pioneer by classmate Lisa Crawford

"I play with Grand Central Corporation. I've been playing with them for two years," said Prince Nelson, senior at Central High. Prince started playing piano at age seven and guitar when he got out of eighth grade.

Prince was born in Minneapolis. When asked, he said, "I was born here, unfortunately." Why unfortunately? "I think it is very hard for a band to make it in this state, even if they're good, mainly because there aren't any big record companies or studios in this state. I really feel that if we would have lived in Los Angeles or New York or some other big city, we would have gotten over by now" [referring to a record contract].

He likes Central a great deal because his music teachers let him work on his own. He is now working with Mr. Bickham, a music teacher at Central, but has been working with Mrs. Doepkes.

He plays several instruments, such as guitar, bass, all keyboards, and drums. He also sings sometimes, which he picked up recently. He played saxophone in seventh grade but gave it up. He regrets he did. He quit playing sax when school ended one summer. He never had time to practice sax anymore when he went back to school. He does not play in the school band. Why? "I really don't have time to make the concerts."

Prince has a brother that goes to Central whose name is Duane Nelson, who is more athletically enthusiastic. He plays on the basketball team and played on the football team. Duane is also a senior.

Prince plays by ear. "I've had about two lessons, but they didn't help much. I think you'll always be able to do what your ear tells you, so just think how great you'd be with lessons also," he said.

"I advise anyone who wants to learn guitar to get a teacher unless they are very musically inclined. One should learn all their scales, too. That is very important," he continued.

Prince would also like to say that his band is in the process of recording an album containing songs they have composed. It should be released during the early part of the summer.

"Eventually I would like to go to college and start lessons again when I'm much older."

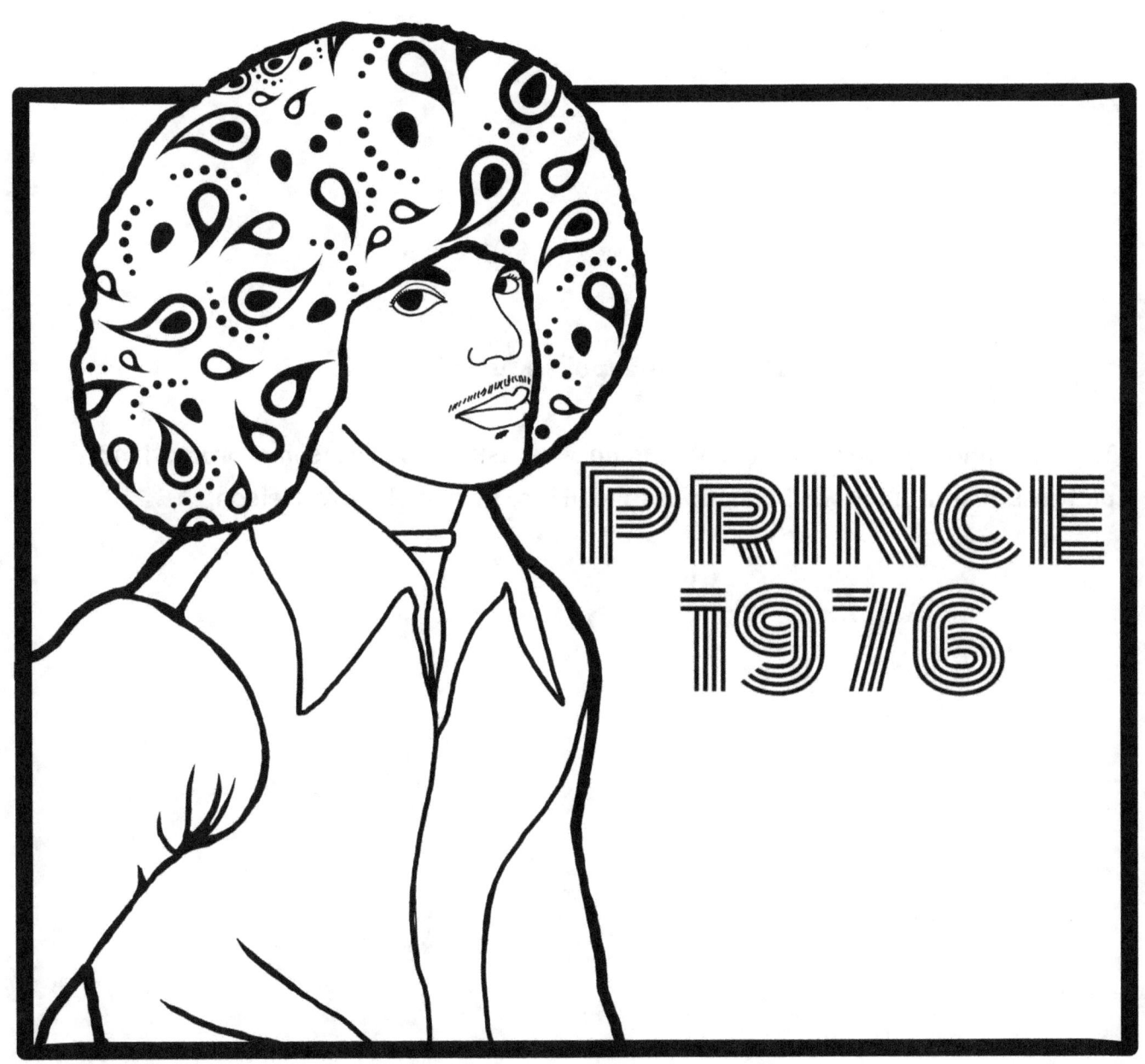

1977 Minneapolis Music Wall

In 1977, photographer Robert Whitman was asked to take some promotional pictures of an unknown Minneapolis musician, Prince Rogers Nelson.

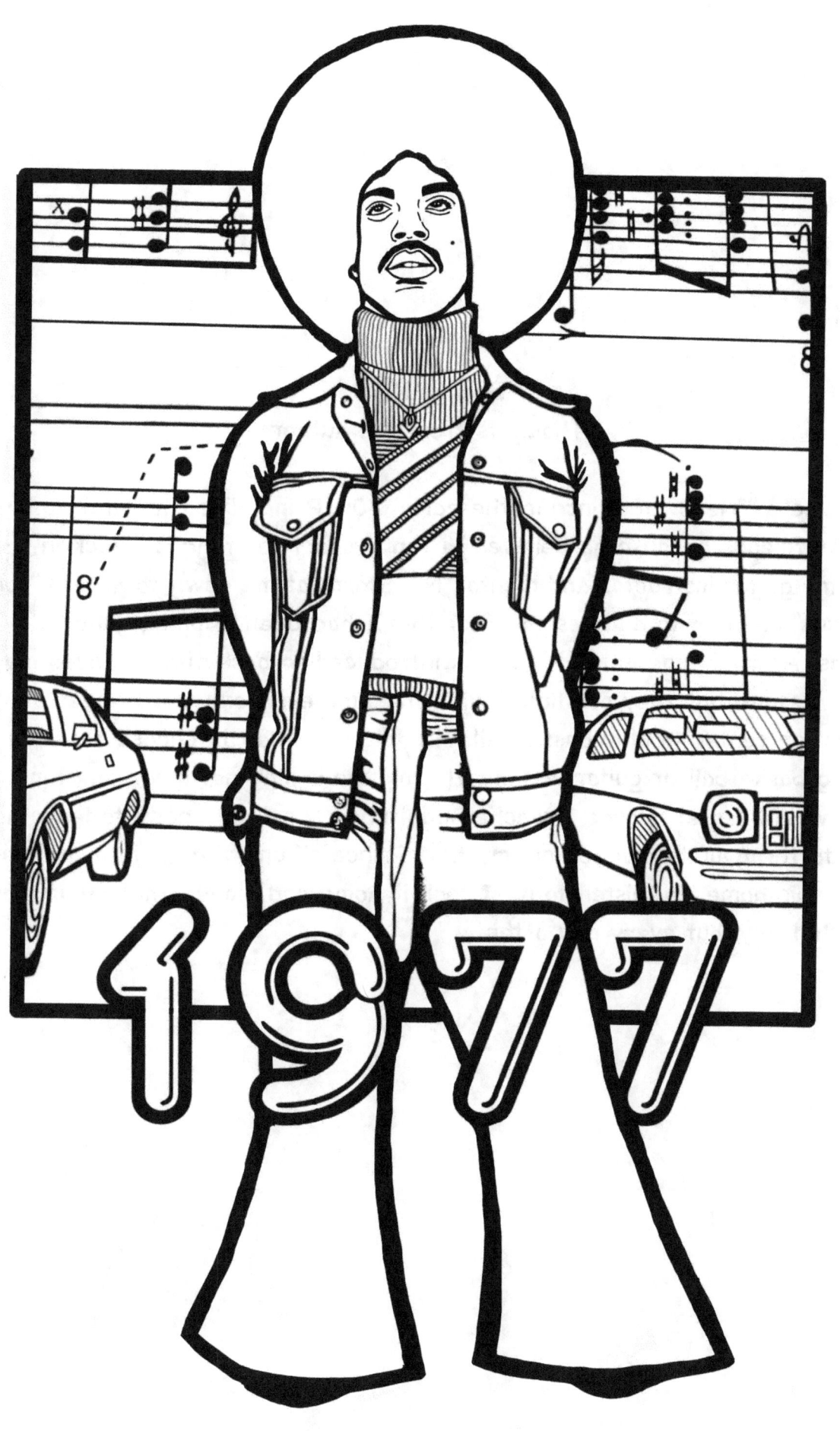

Prince 1979
Thoughts from the author

I became a "friend" of Prince in the early '80s. Prince liked to refer to his fans as friends because he believed "a fan is short for fanatic." Back in the '80s, my guitar instructor and mentor, Nic Starr sat me down to have a "come to Jesus" meeting to address the fact that I had been skipping guitar lessons. At that time in my life I was introduced to basketball. I loved my guitar lessons, but they conflicted with the time everyone would meet at the recreation center to play basketball. Nic told me I had to choose between playing basketball or guitar lessons. He told me it may not mean anything now, but I would regret it once I reached adulthood. As I got ready to leave and walk to the gym, he handed me my first Prince album titled Prince. He said, "Take this home, and listen to it." I took it home and played that album not only that day, but every day after.

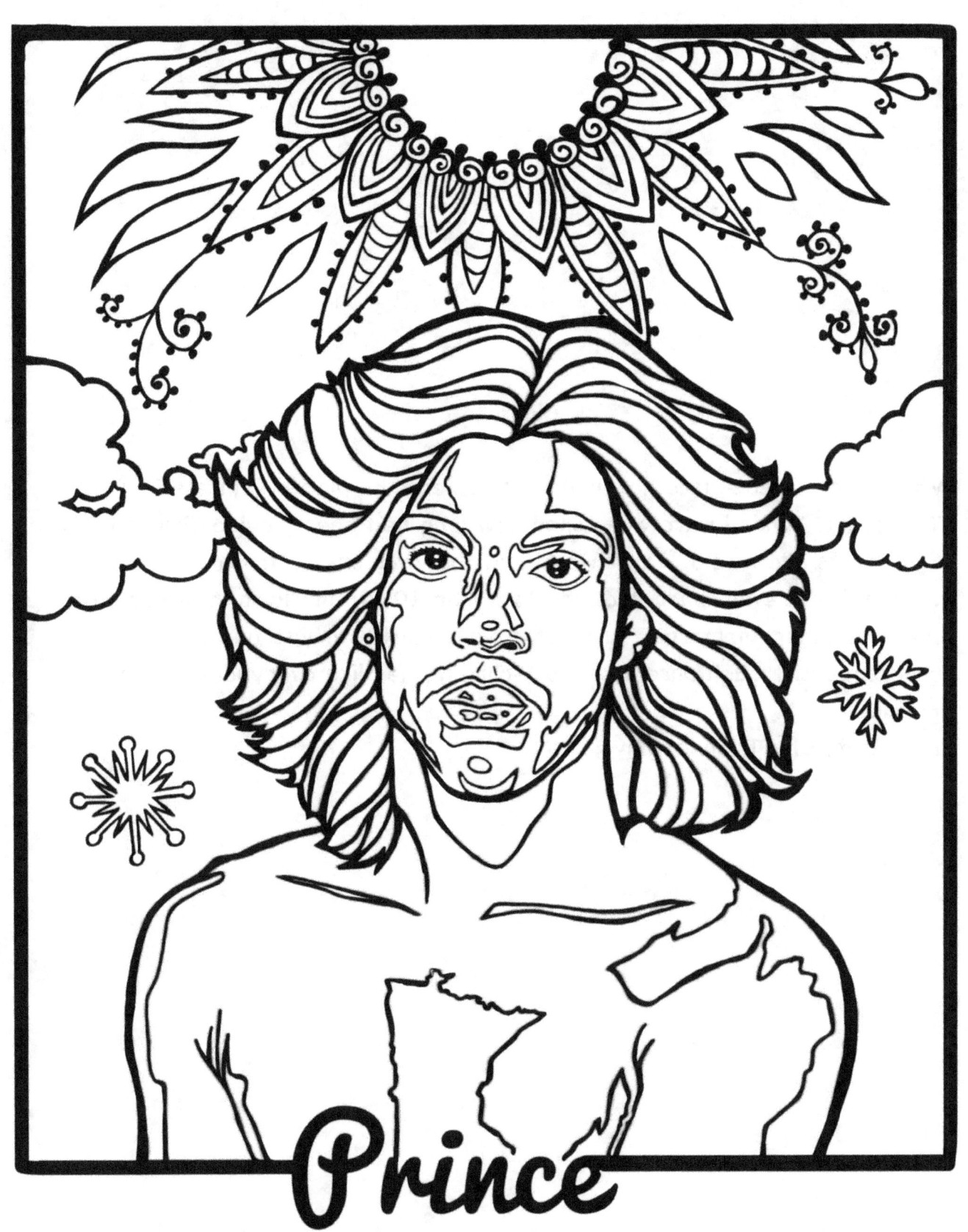

Prince

Dick Clark Interview

When Clark asked Prince how many instruments he played Prince said, "Thousands." When Prince was asked how long he'd been playing, Prince raised four fingers. Clark said, "I've always said that was one of the most difficult interviews I've ever conducted, and I've done 10,000 musician interviews. He's an extraordinary performer and not a particularly verbose one in public conversations, though once you're off-camera, he's like everybody else, very normal."

Jon Bream, Star Tribune, May 3, 2013

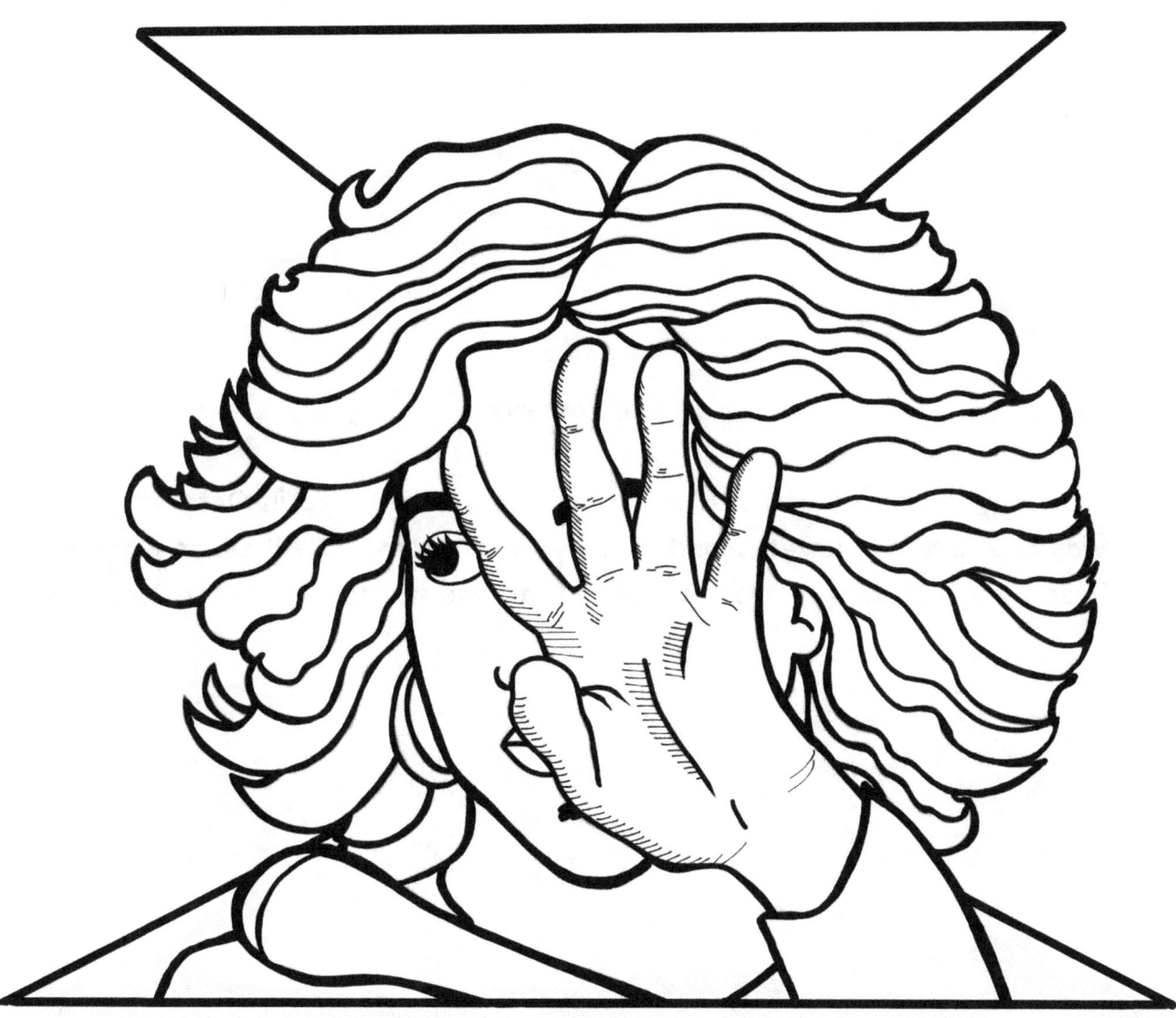

Controversy

Controversy is Prince's 4th studio album that was released in October 1981. It was recorded at Sunset Sound in Hollywood, California. All songs were written by Prince except "Do Me, Baby" that was written by Andre Cymone.

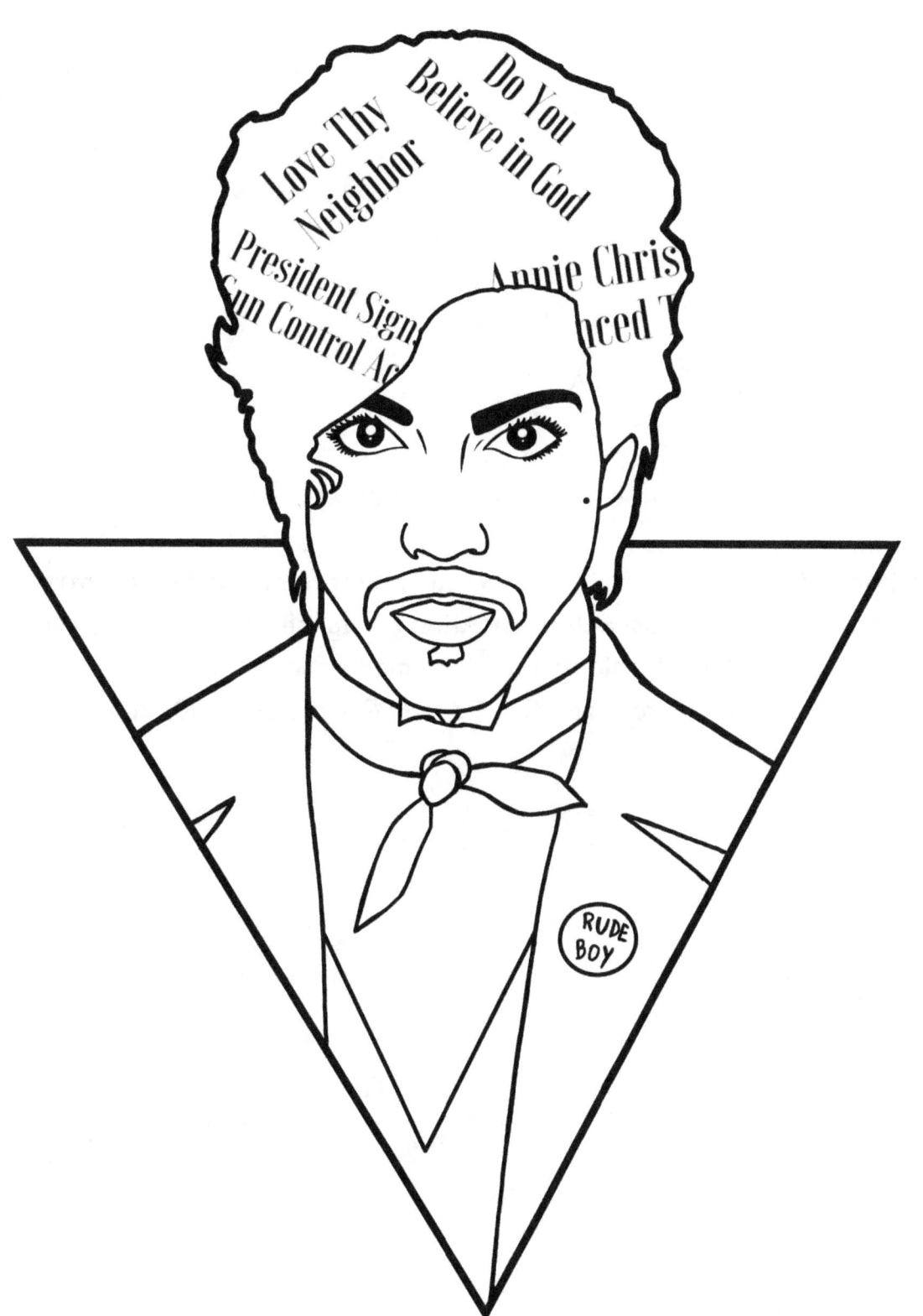

Purple Rain

On July 27, 1984, Purple Rain hit movie theaters across the country. It is reported that Prince gave director Albert Magnoli 100 songs for him to select for the movie. Magnoli selected 12 that made the movie.
Newsweek Special Commemorative Edition, Prince, June 30, 2016.

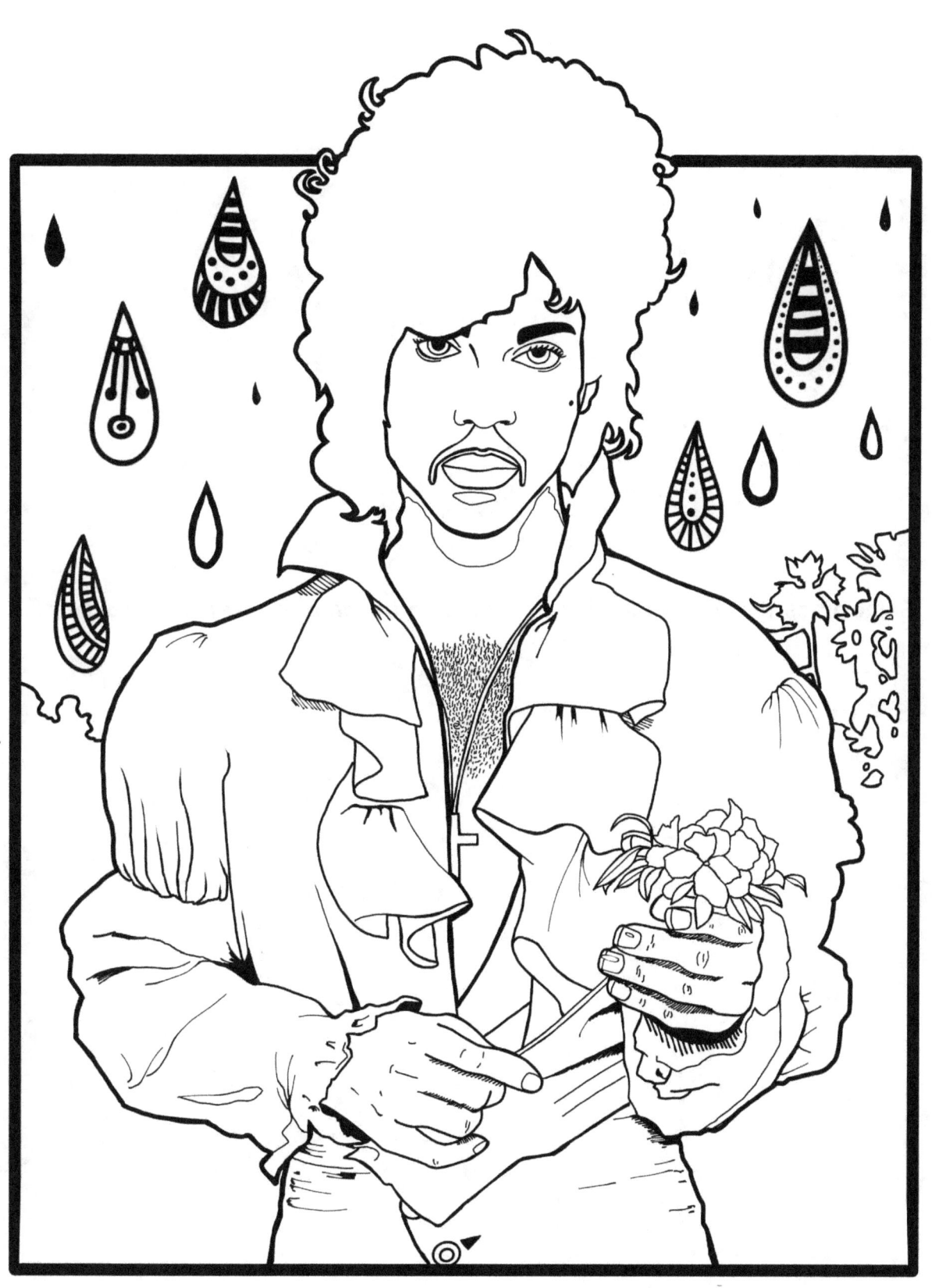

"Sometimes it takes years for a person to become an overnight success."
Prince

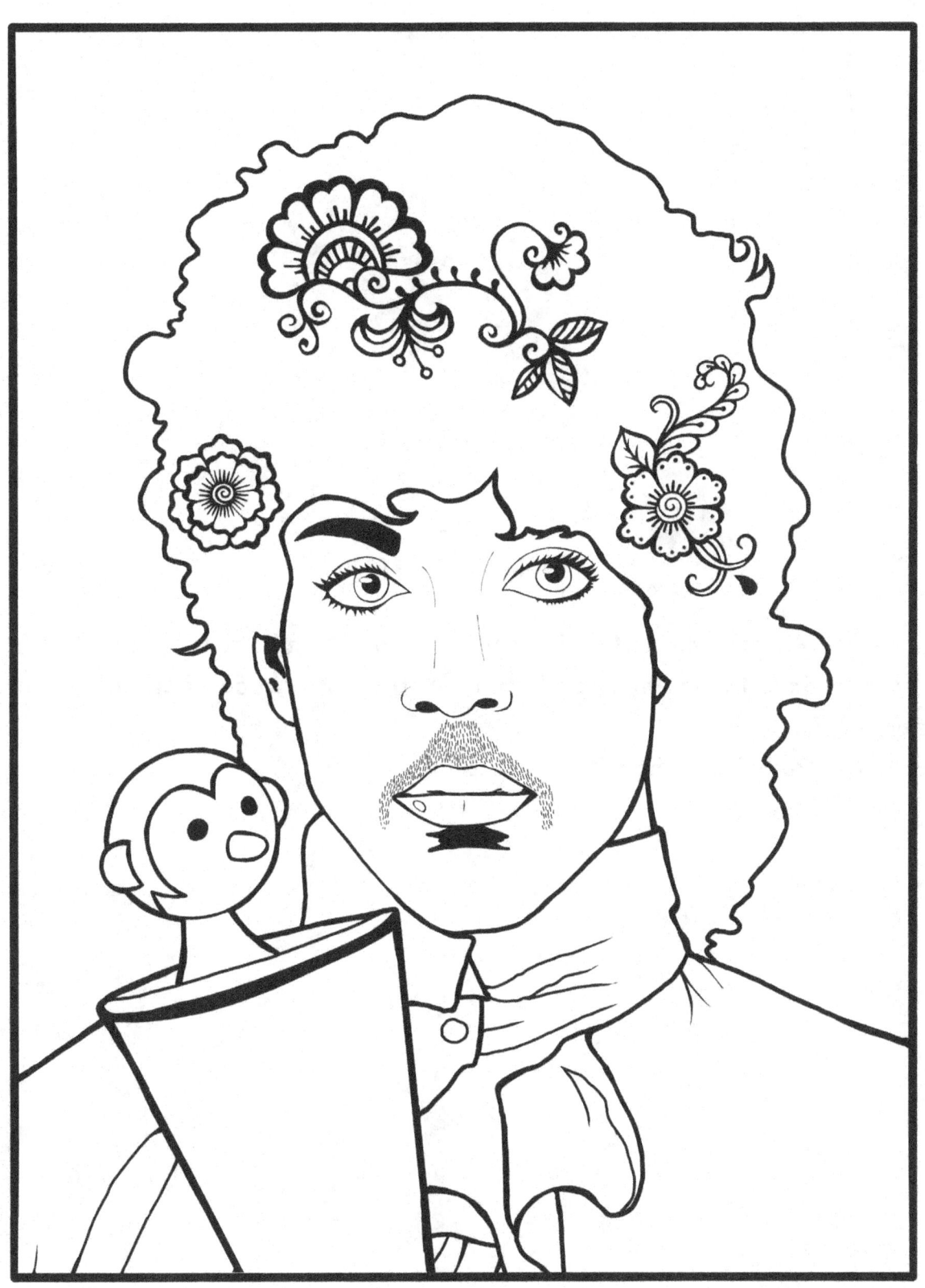

Raspberry Beret

"Raspberry Beret is packed with small, everyday details that give it the flavor of a short story by an American author, such as Sherwood Anderson or John Cheever."
Alan Di Perna, Prince: The Ultimate Tribute

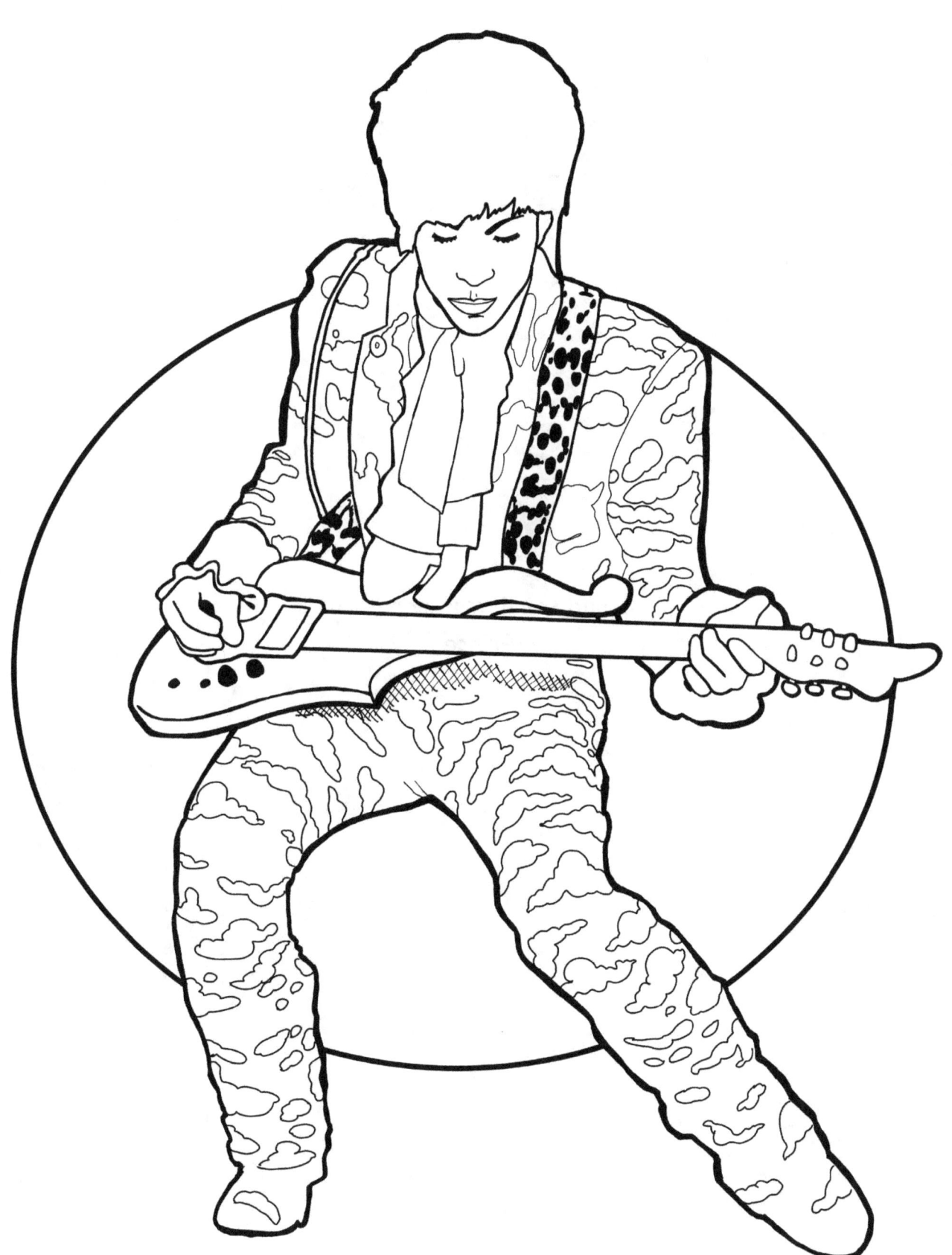

"A strong spirit transcends rules."
Prince

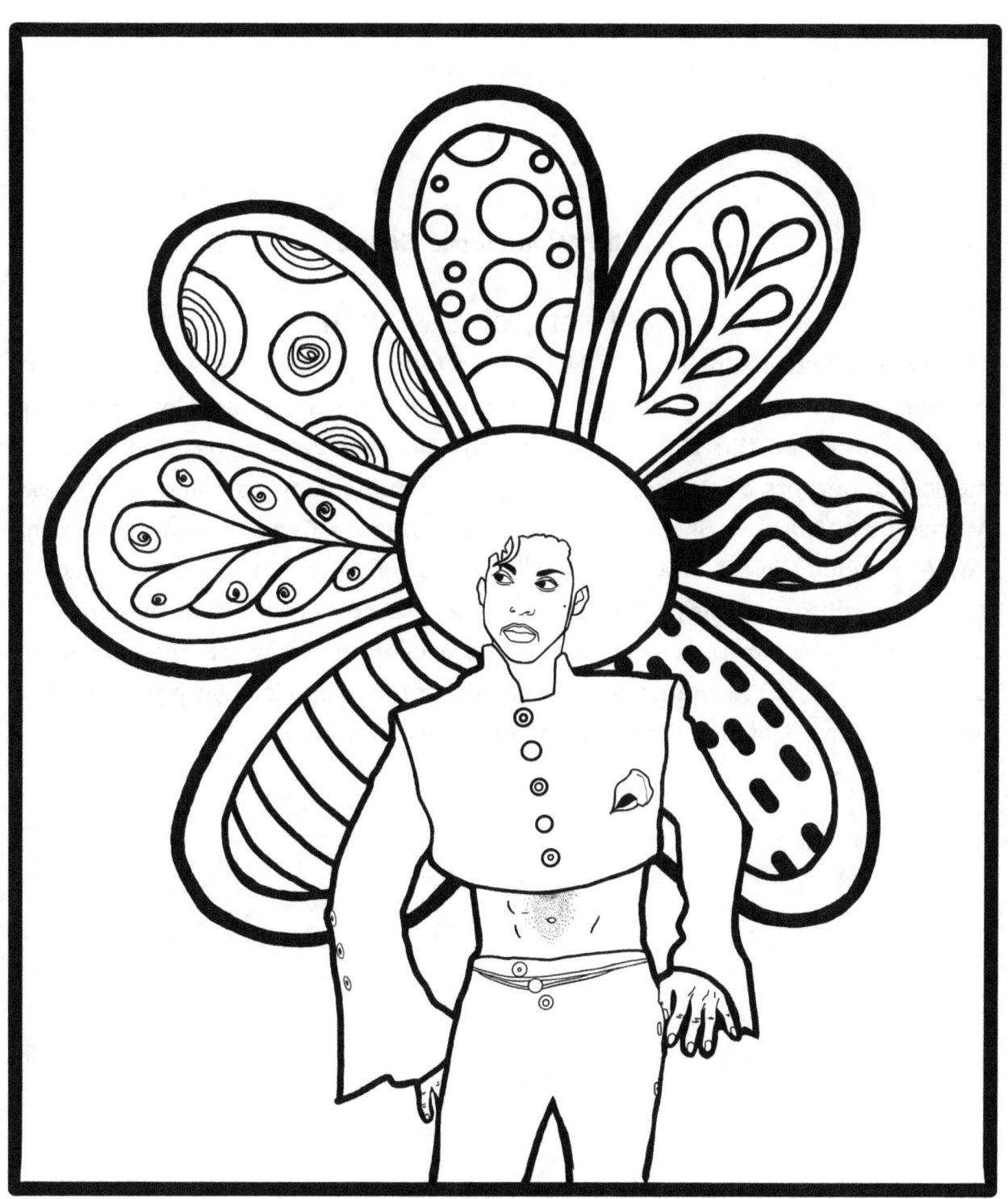

The Minneapolis Sound

Minnesota is not just the land of 10,000 lakes; it's the home of "The Minneapolis Sound." In the late 1970s, The Minneapolis Sound was pioneered by Prince and today is a sub-genre of funk rock with elements of synth-pop and new wave. In the 1980s, its popularity became even bigger thanks to the musical adherents of Prince, as well as The Time, Jimmy Jam and Terry Lewis, Morris Day, Vanity 6, Sheila E, Jesse Johnson, Andre Cymone, Dez Dickerson, and Alexander O'Neal. The Minneapolis Sound influenced many artists back then and still does today. Bruno Mars even incorporated The Minneapolis Sound into his song "Uptown Funk." While accepting his award for best album on January 28, 2018, he gave a shout-out to Minneapolis' own producers/writers Jimmy Jam and Terry Lewis for being an influence.

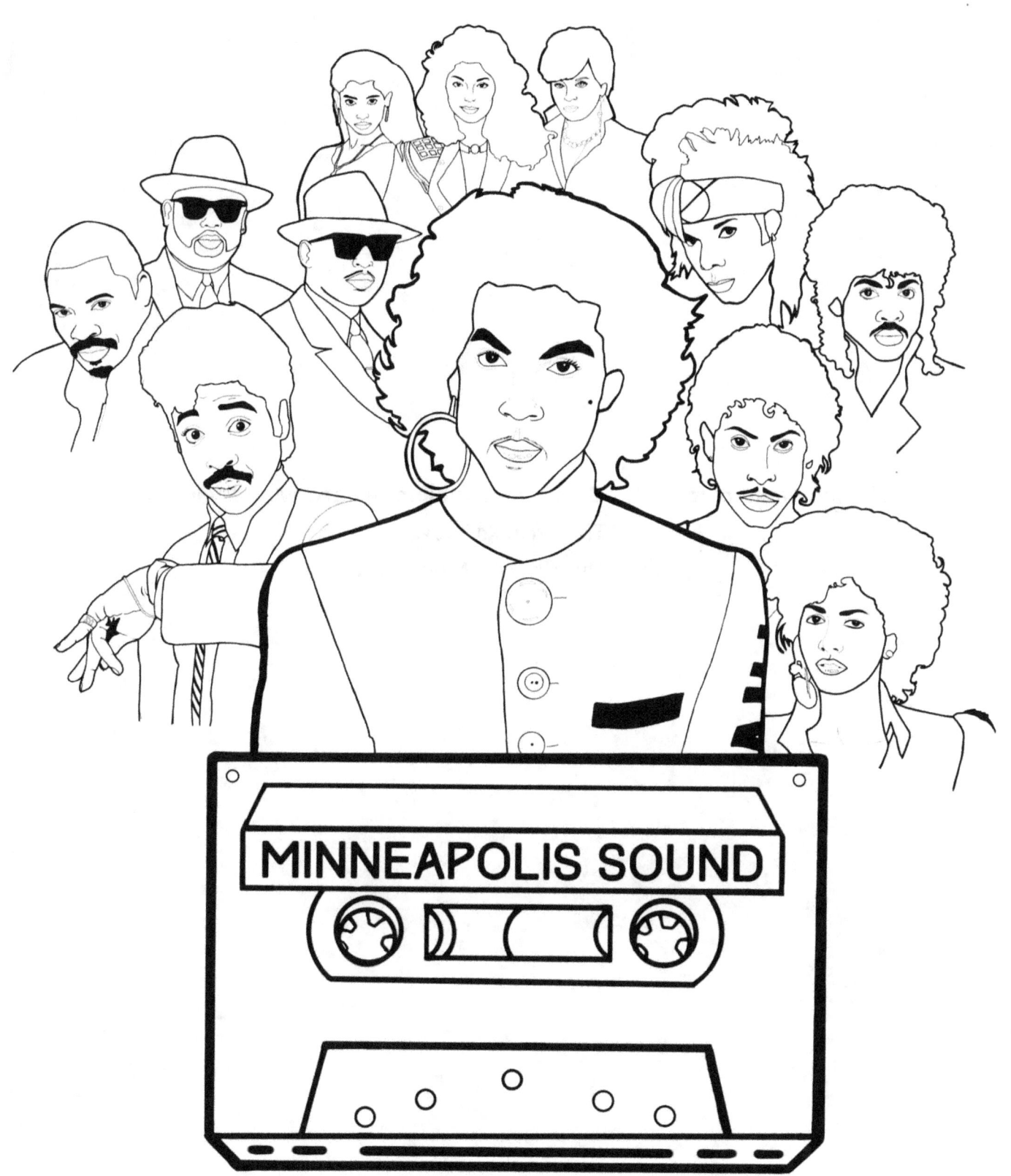

"If you wanted to buy a Sam Cooke a'blum, where would you go?"
"The wrecka stow."
Under the Cherry Moon, 1986

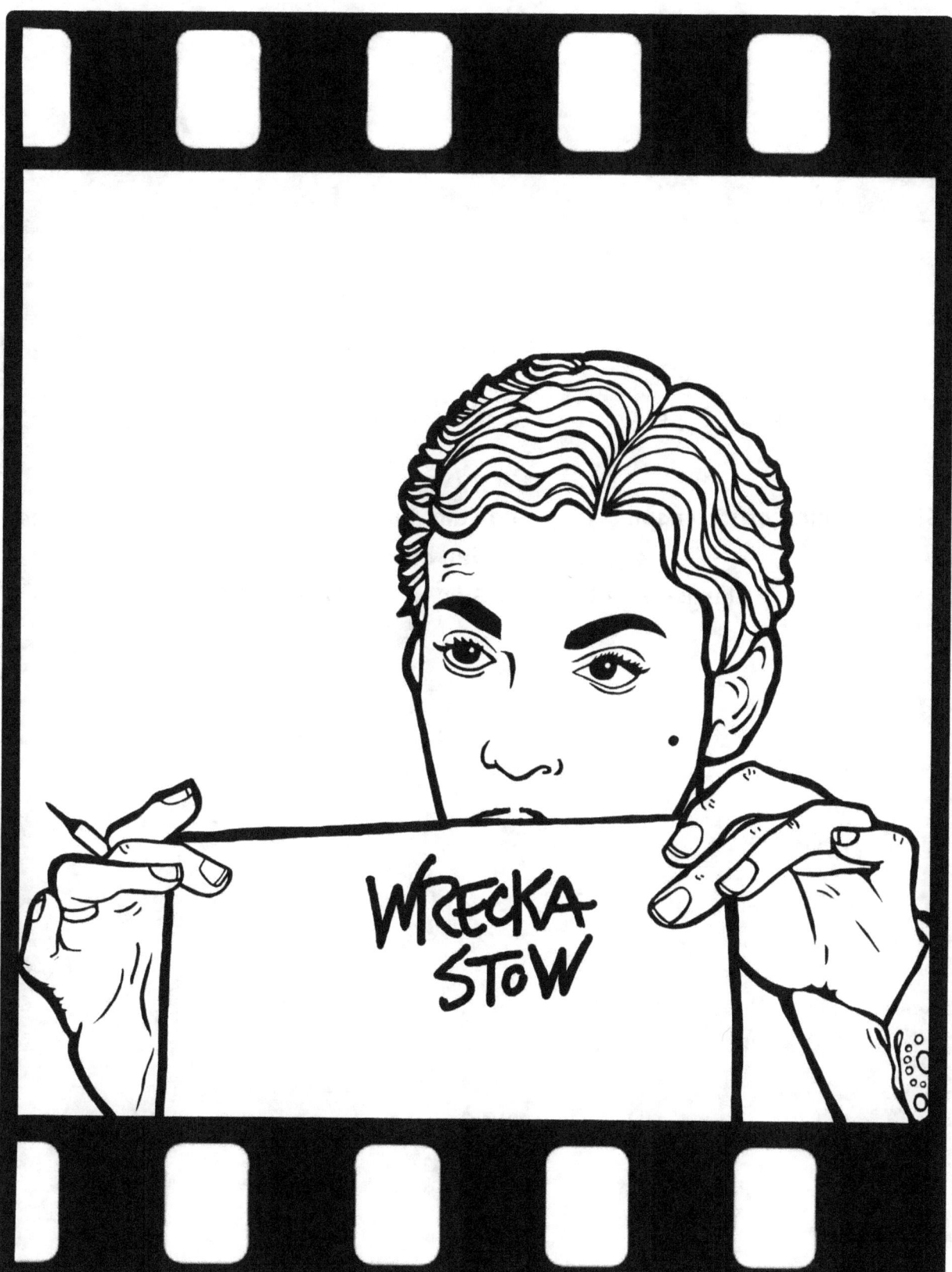

"Starfish and coffee; maple syrup and jam. Butterscotch clouds, a tangerine, and a side order of ham..."
"Starfish and Coffee", Sign o' the Times, 1987

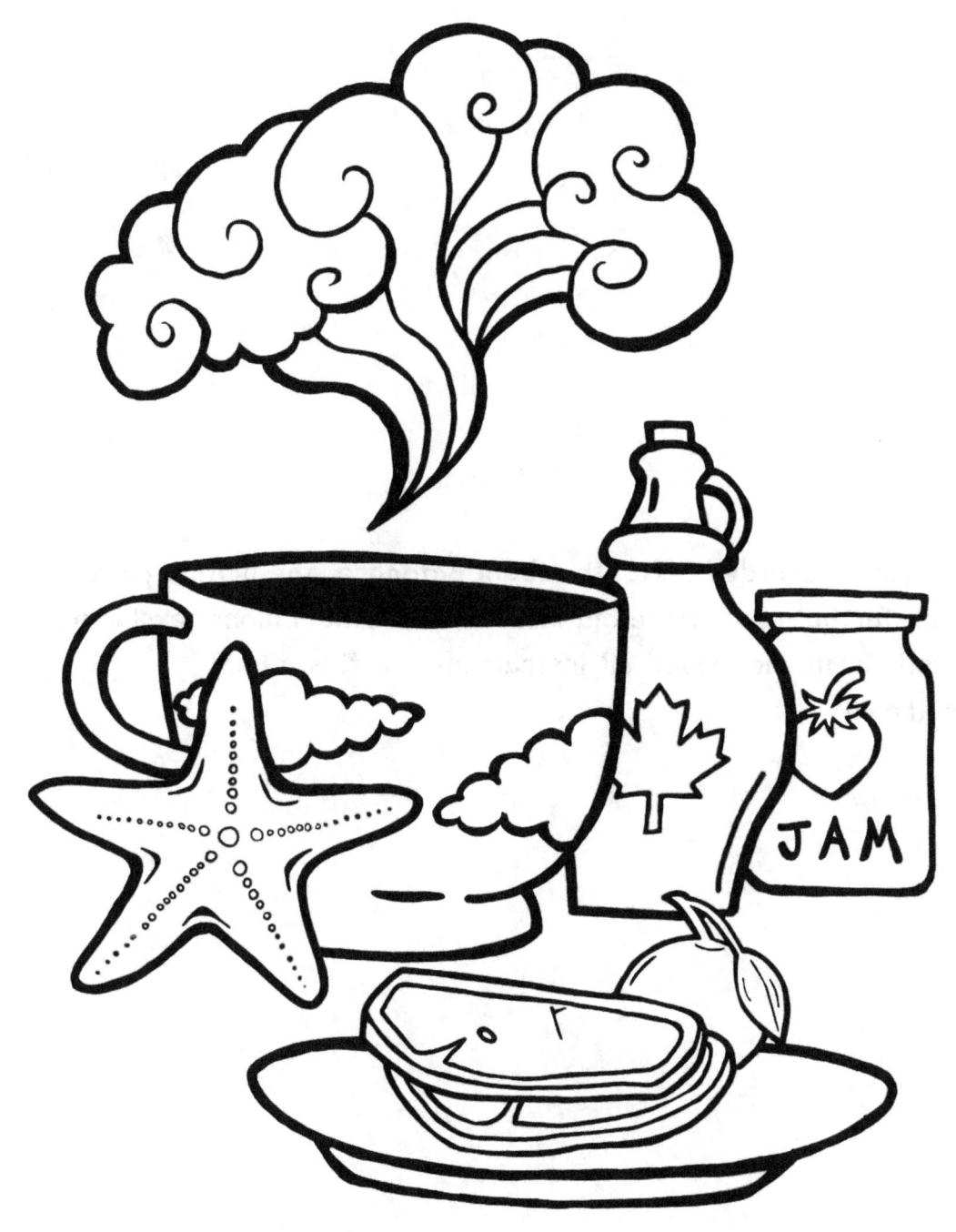

STARFISH & COFFEE

Batdance

In 1989, Prince recorded his 11th album Batdance, the motion picture soundtrack for Batman. Prince did most of this album alone, excluding some background vocals. He played all instruments on this album.
Princevault.com

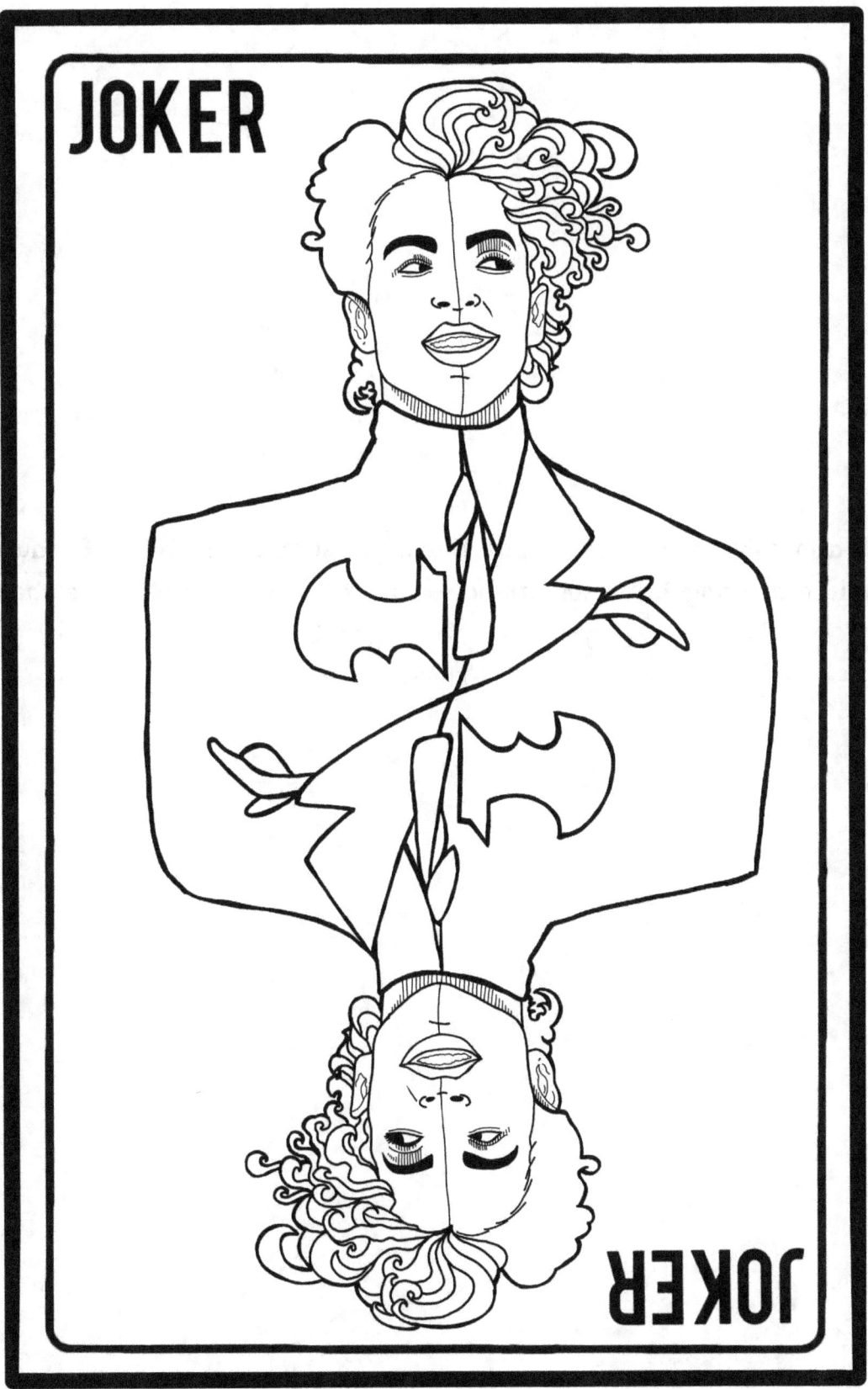

"I had a massive ego. Massive. But that's not such a bad thing. Because at least you're aspiring to be something — you consider yourself great because you want to be great."
Prince

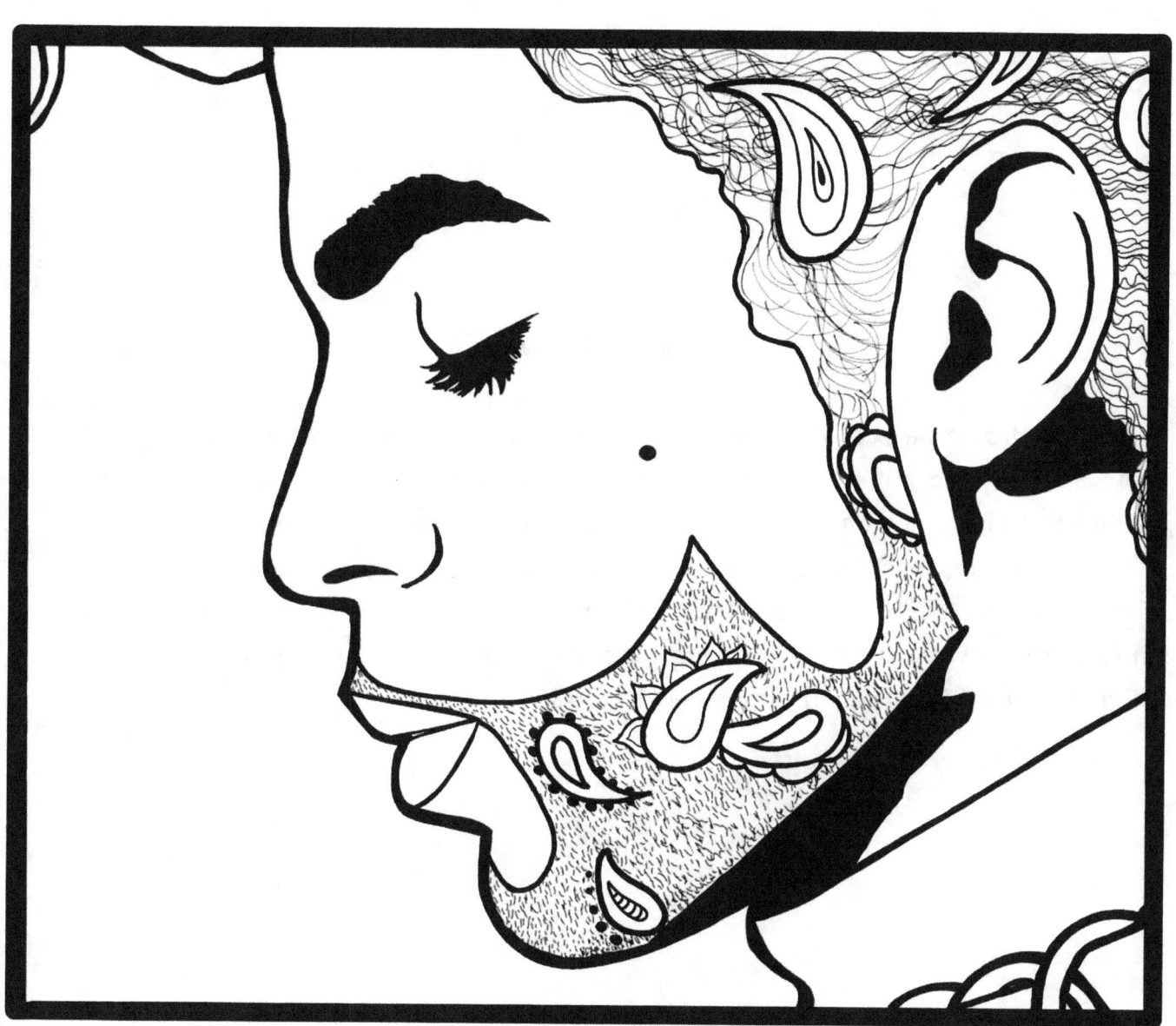

James Brown

"James Brown played a big influence on my style. When I was about 10 years old, my stepdad put me on the stage with him, and I danced a little bit with him until the bodyguard took me off. The reason why I like James Brown is because on my backstage, on my way out, I saw some of the finest dancing girls I ever seen in my life. And, I think, and I respect, he influenced me by his control over his group, dancing girls, his apples, and his oranges."
Prince's First Television Interview—MTV 1985

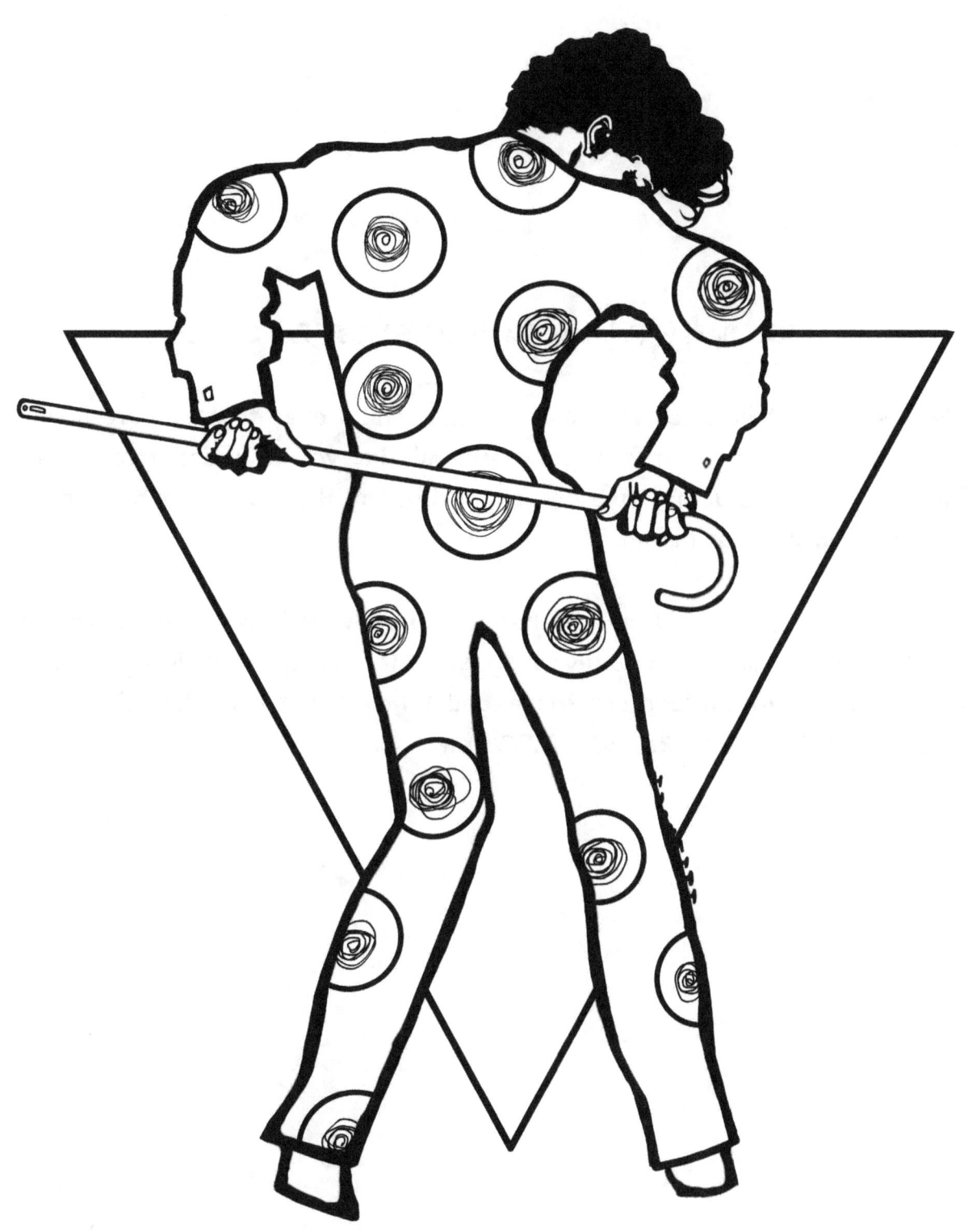

Kim Berry, Prince's Personal Stylist for 28 Years

"He wore more hairstyles then most women would ever try. He wore it all the way across the spectrum from pony tails all the way to wraps, from cuts to finger waves so he didn't have no boundaries. For the most part he was pretty much laid back about his hair.

He knew what he wanted, and he had a feel of what he wanted himself to look like. He would let me do my thing, so that was the beautiful part about it. He would throw an idea out there, and I would just run with it."
By Lauren Effron, April 22, 2016 ABC News

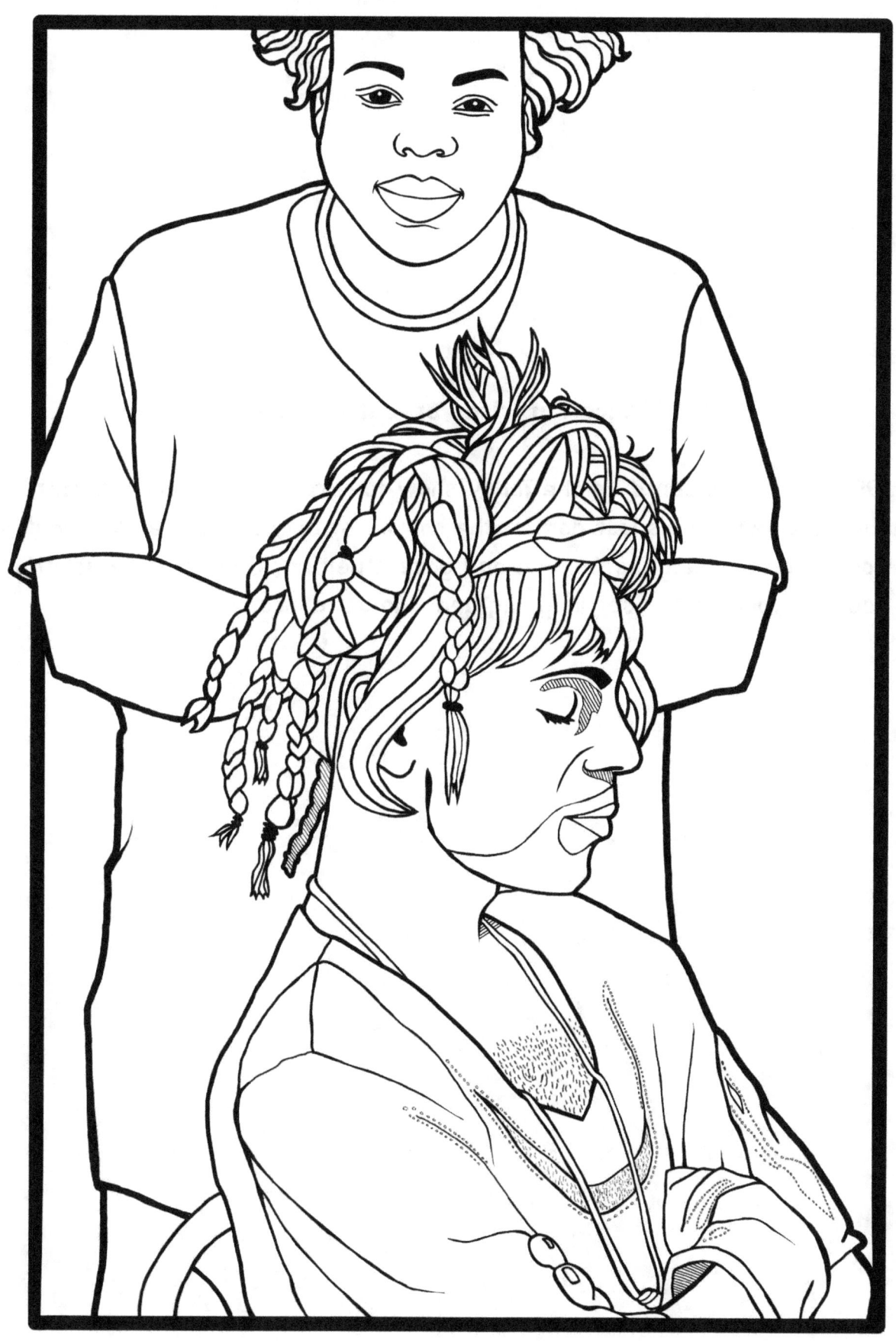

Prince Surprises Bryant Gumbel

In 1997, Prince appeared on the Today show to surprise TV anchor Bryant Gumbel to celebrate his last day on the show. Not only did he perform, but he also appeared dressed like Gumbel and gave a perfect Gumbel impersonation. He had everyone on the set laughing and Gumbel almost in tears.

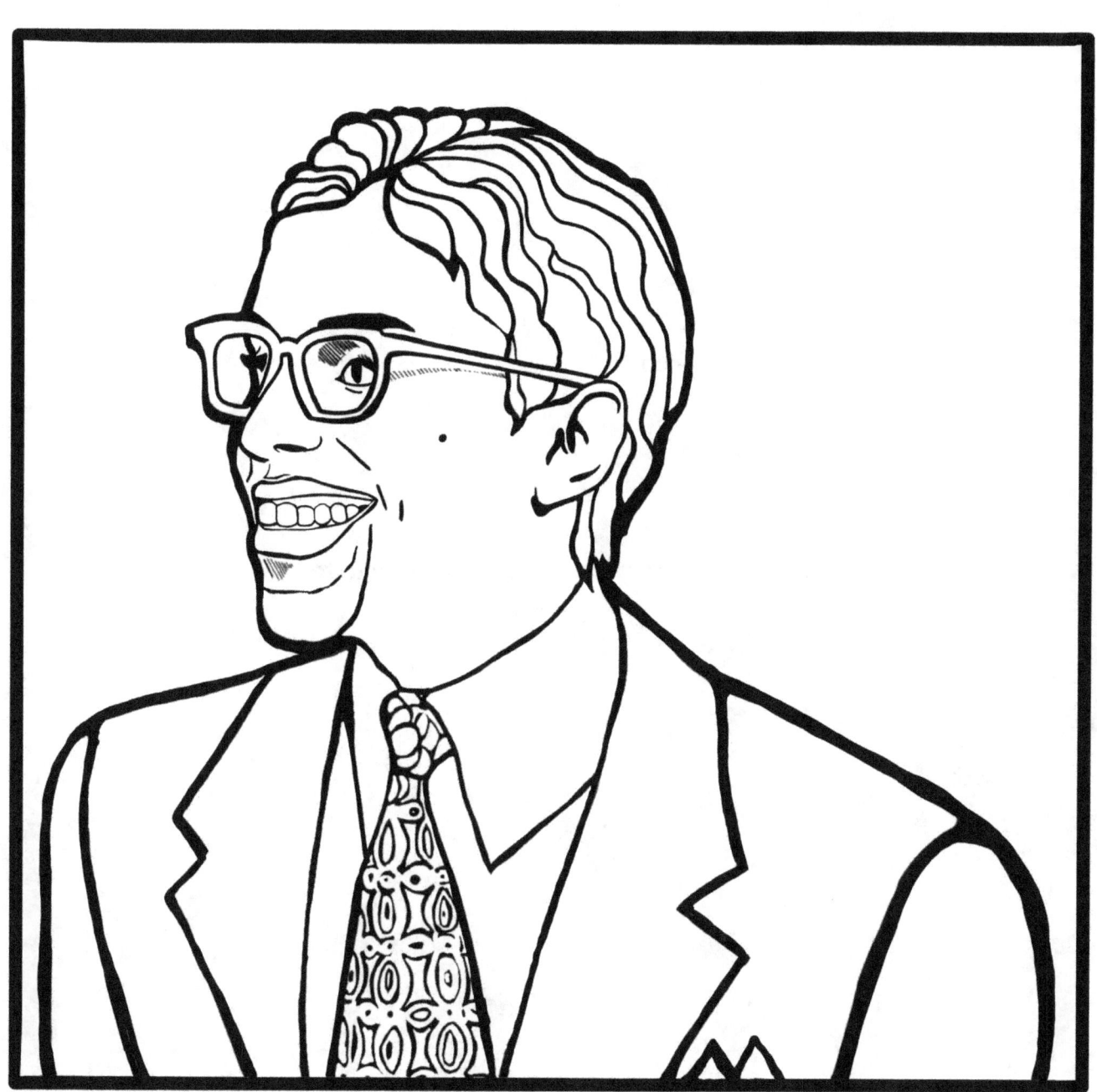

"If you don't own your master tape, your master owns you."
Prince

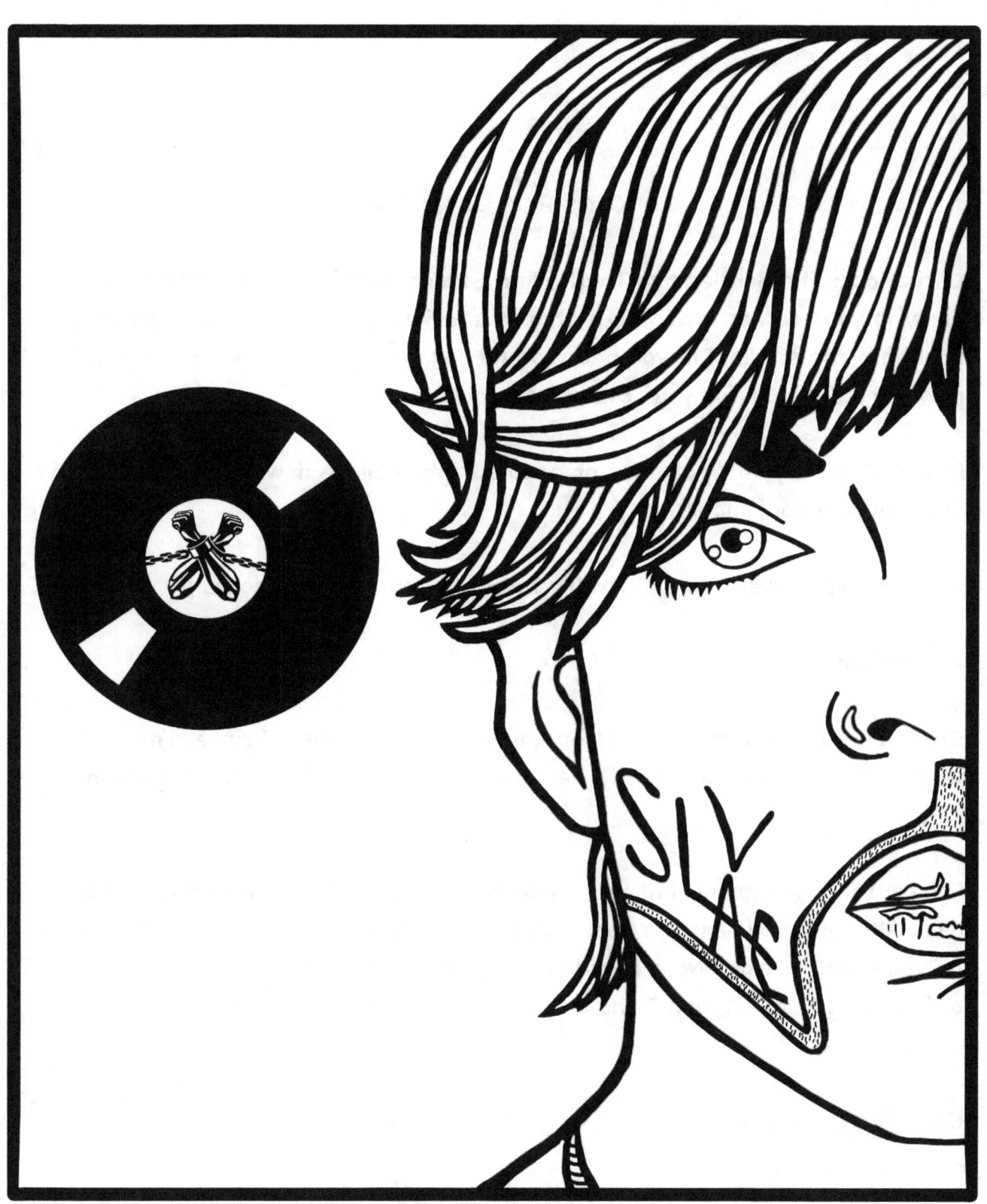

Chris Rock Interview

Chris Rock: The Beatles had The Rolling Stones. Elvis had Jerry Lee Lewis. Early in your career, who was it that you looked at and said. Oh, I got to get back into the studio. Did you hear so and so? Let's get into the studio right now. Who did that for you? Everyone's got somebody.

Prince: Contrary to what a lot of people might believe it was never, somebody that was my contemporary.

Chris: It was never like any rivalry between you and Mr. Jackson?

Prince: Not to me, no.

Chris: I love this story of you, you know, there's all these Prince, I'm sorry, well that's the guy you used to be. There's this story of you turning down "Bad."

Prince: Well, you know that Wesley Snipes character? That would have been me. All right now, you run that video in your mind. The first line in that song is "your butt is mine." Now, I said who gonna sing that to who, cause you sho ain't singing it to me, and I sho ain't singing it to you. So right there we have a problem.

Chris Rock, 1997 VH

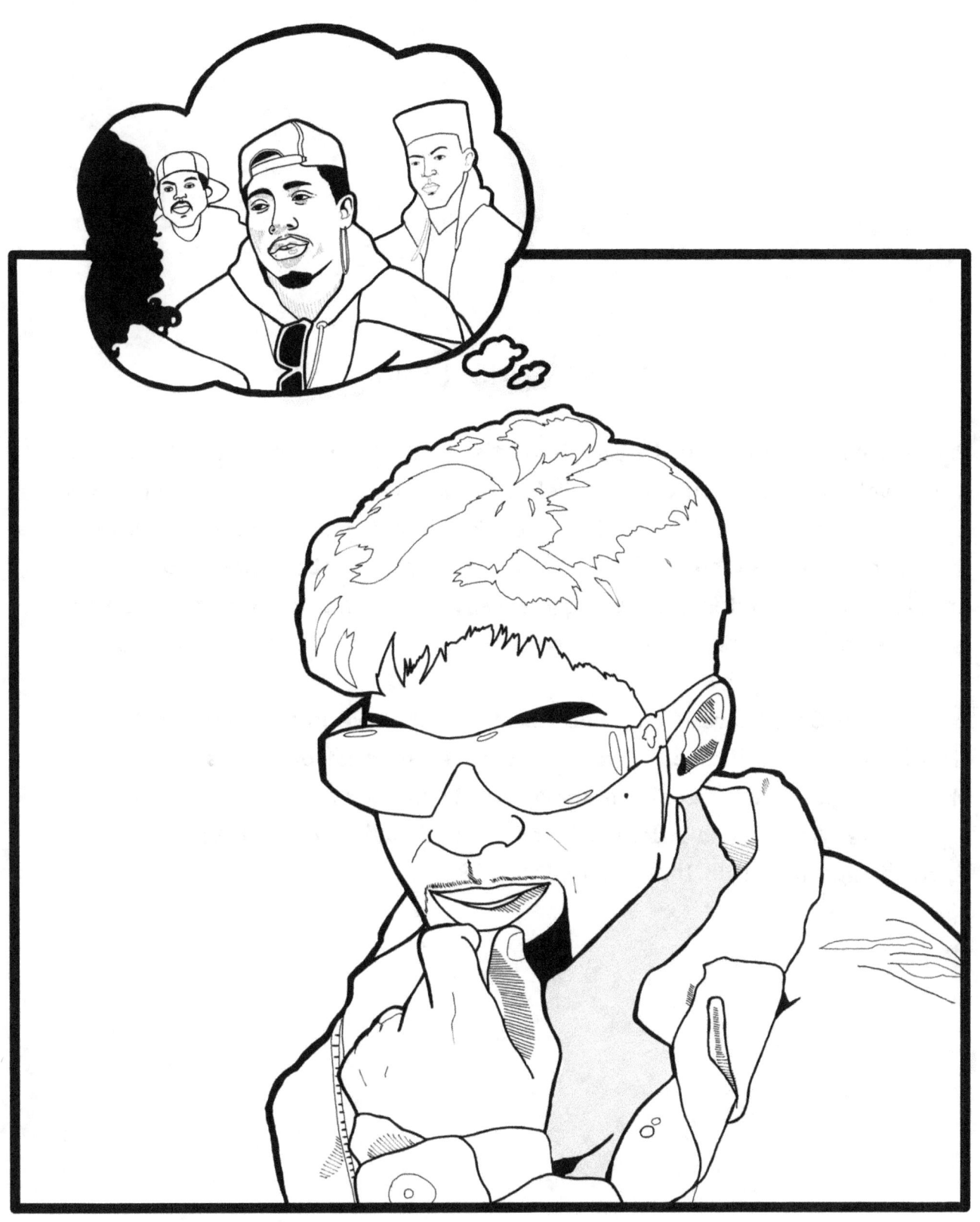

Prince's Spiritual Beliefs

Prince was raised a Seventh-Day Adventist, but later in his career he became a Jehovah's Witness. You can just listen to his lyrics and know that Prince was a man devoted to God. "I Would Die For You" is not a song about two lovers, it's a song about God's love for us. "Let's Go Crazy" is about Jesus. Back then artists were restricted from using the word God in music so he replaced the lyrics, with "Crazy" representing God and the "Elevator" representing Satan.

I believe in God. There is only one God, and I believe in the afterworld. Hopefully, we will all see it. I've been accused of a lot of things contrary to this, and I just want people to know that I am very sincere in my beliefs, and I pray every night, and I don't ask for much. I just say thank you.
Prince's First Television Interview—MTV 1985

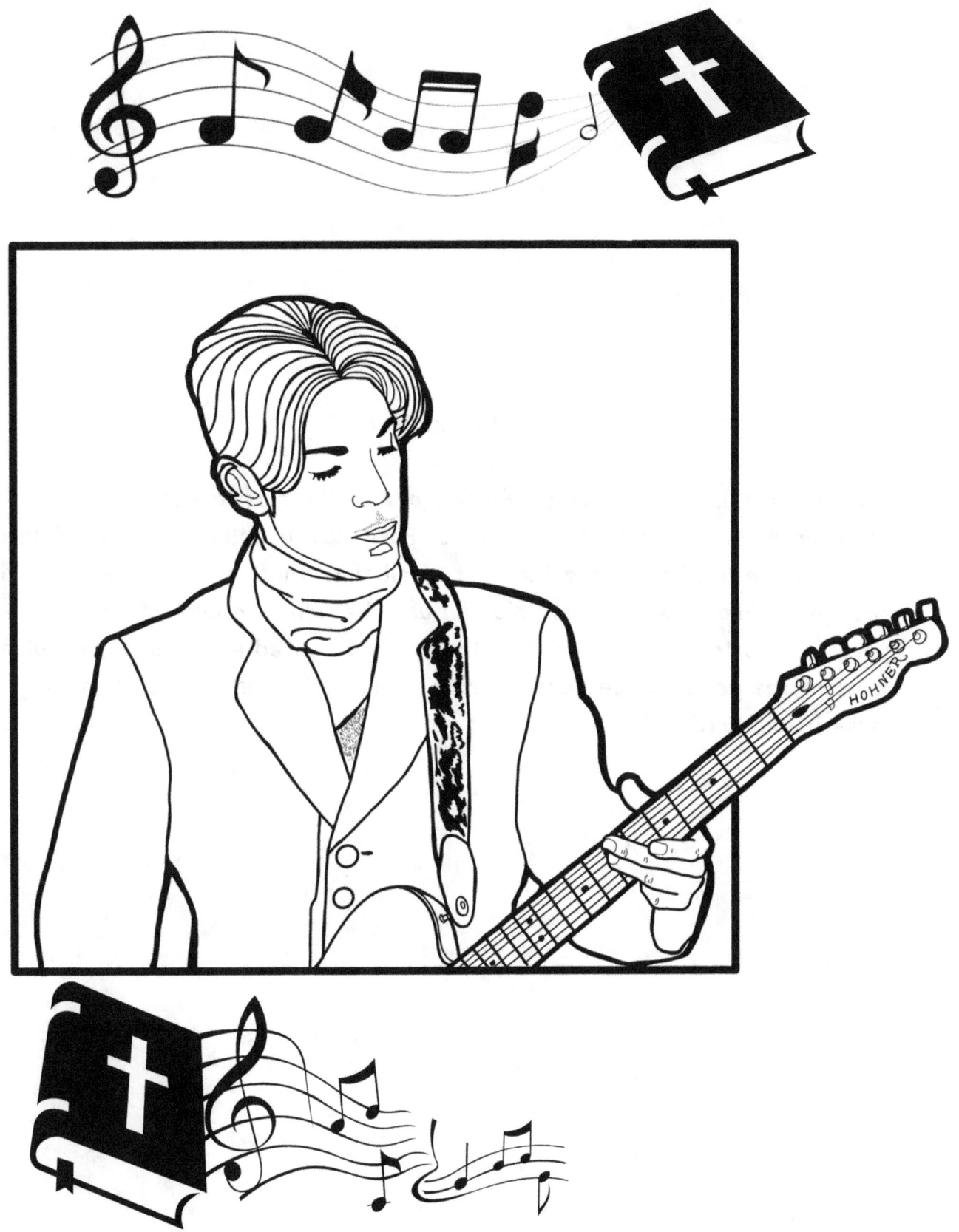

Super Bowl

On February 4, 2007, Prince performed one of the most mesmerizing preferences in the Miami rain for Super Bowl XLI at Dolphin Stadium. Prince's performance has been rated the best of all time. Most artists would have not thought to improvise as Prince did and use the rain as a part of his performance to make it more epic. The producer asked Prince if he was okay to start the performance because of the rain, and Prince asked, "Can you make it rain harder?"

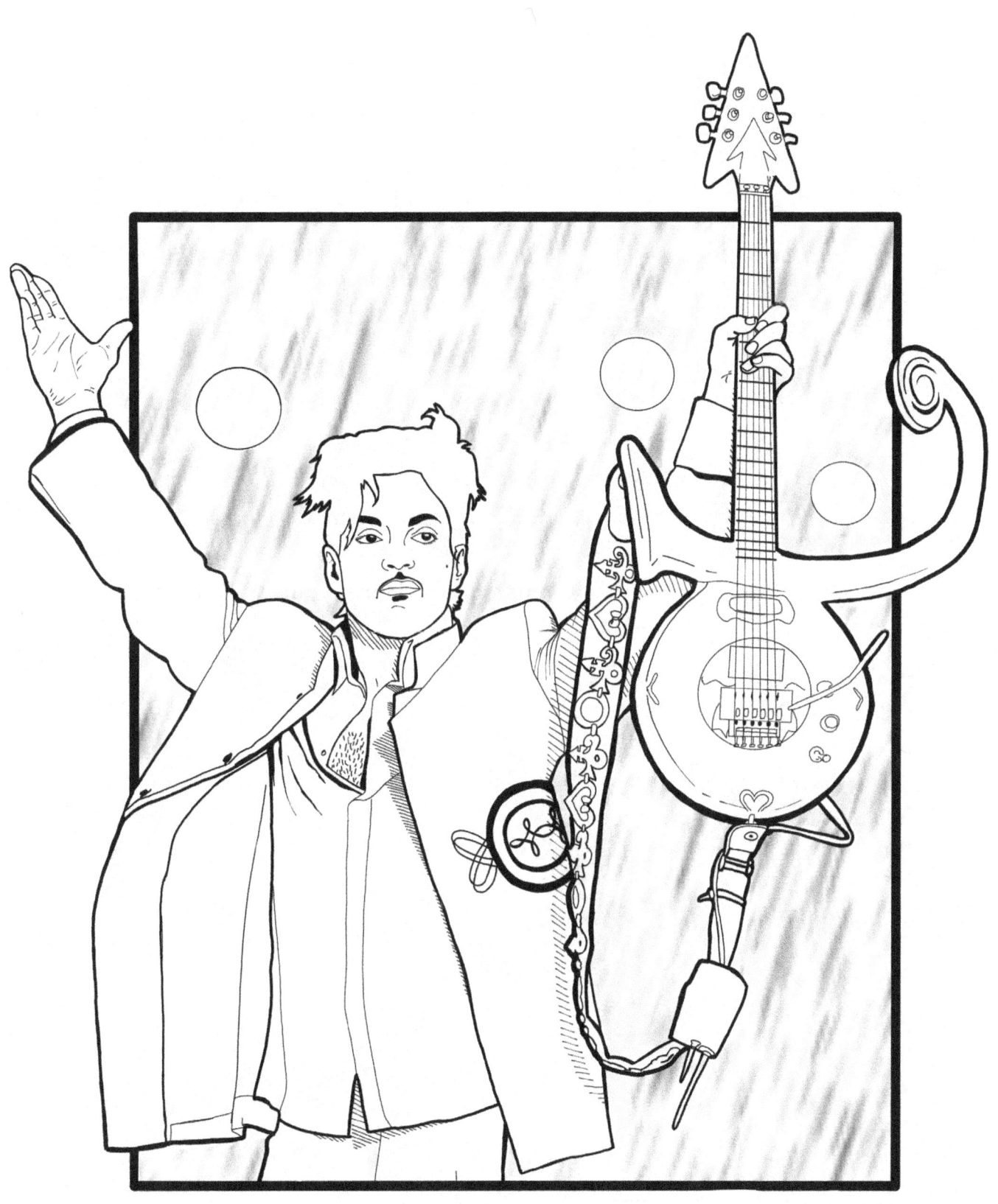

Prince and Kim Kardashian

When Prince brought you on stage to dance, you'd better dance

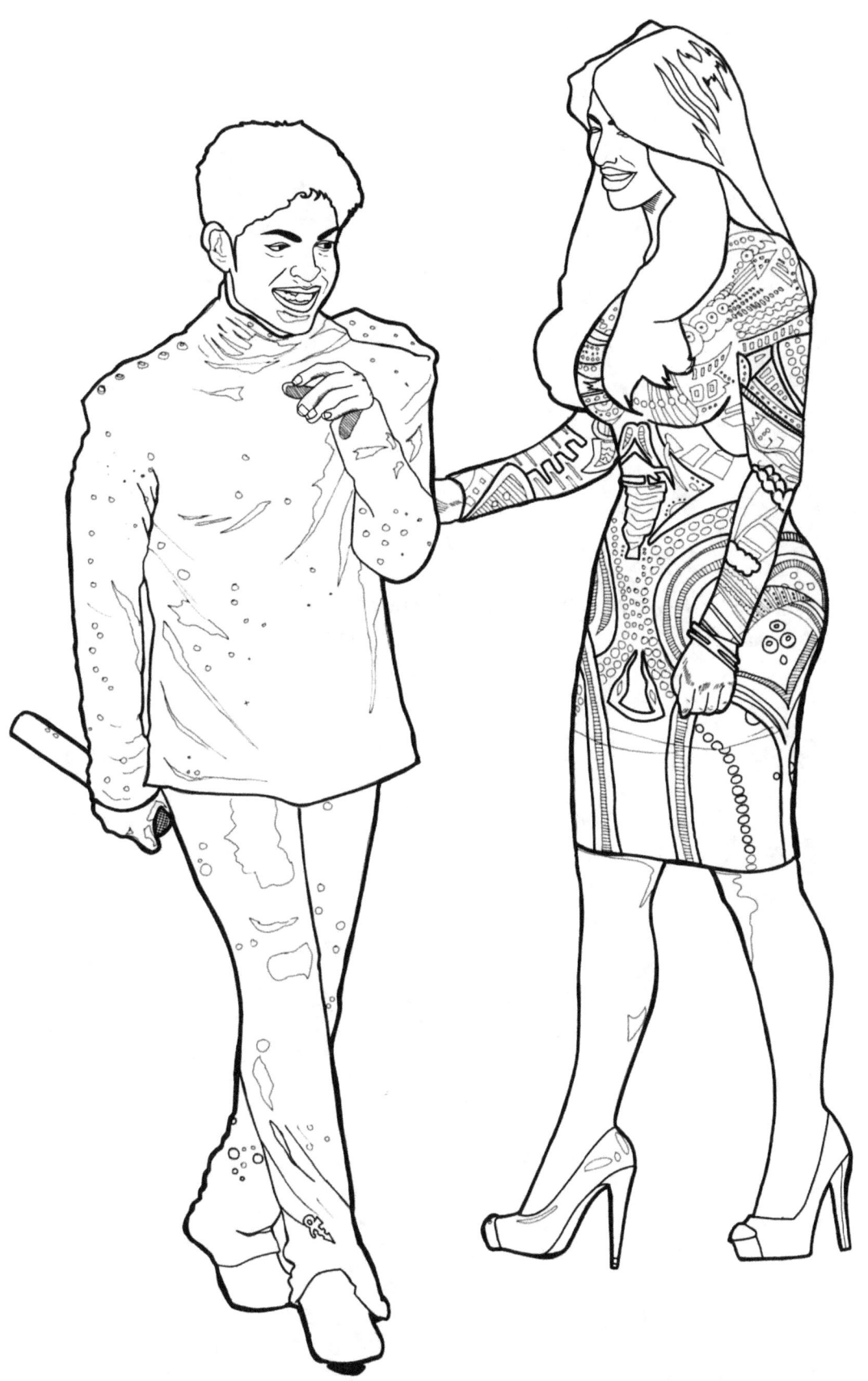

"Always cry for love, never cry for pain."
Prince

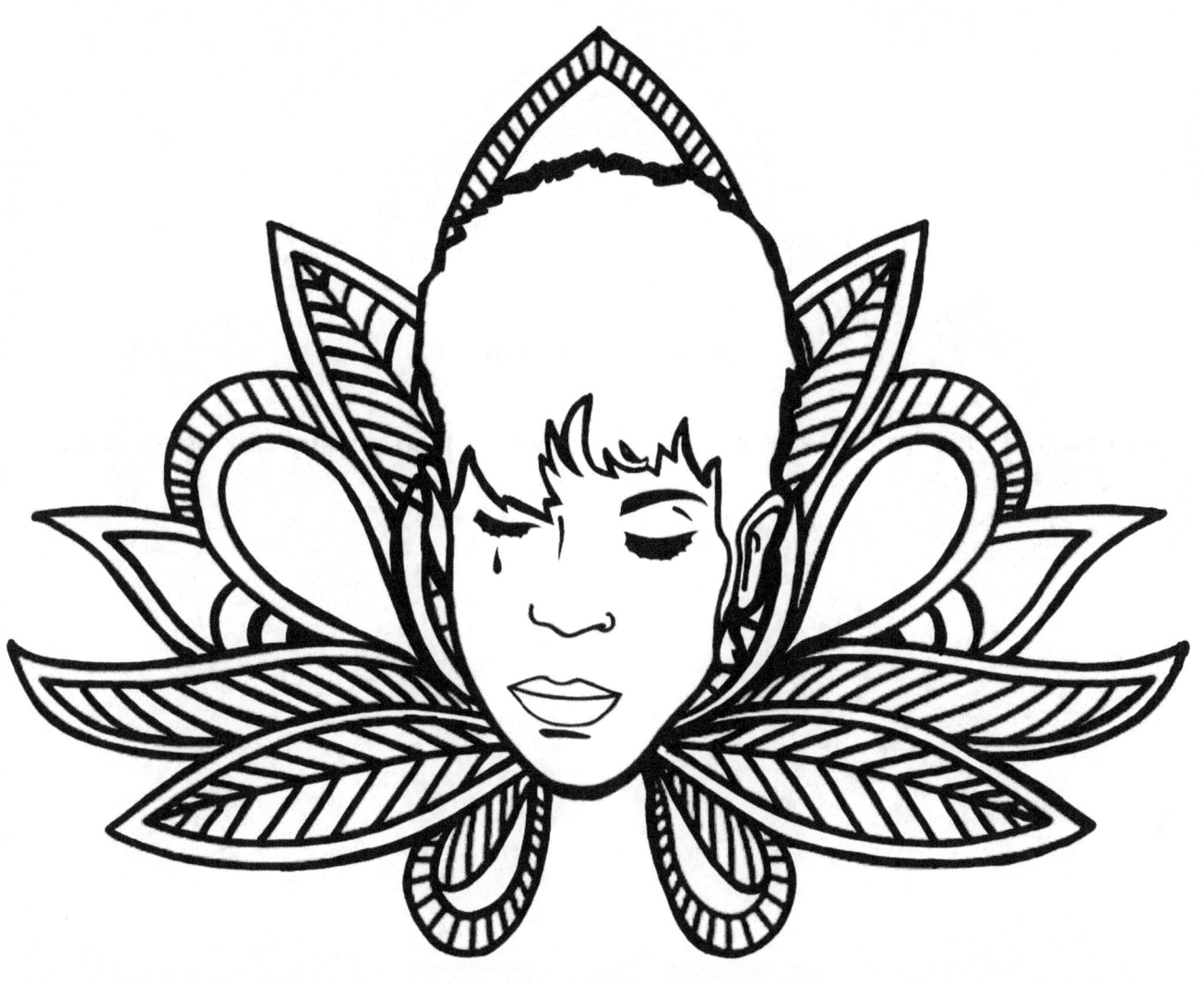

Fashion Evolution

Prince had an array of stylish looks that were often daring, but never dull.

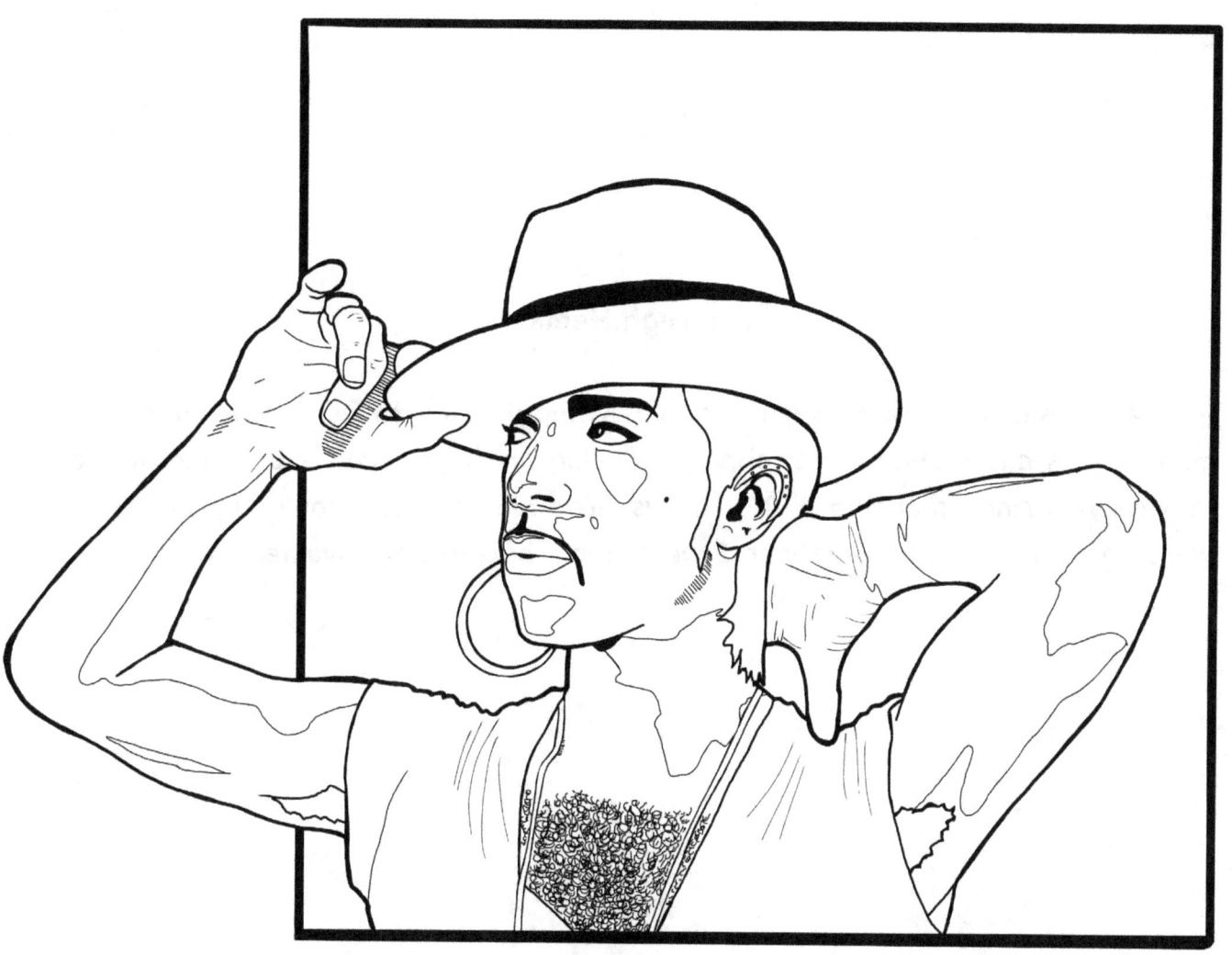

The High Heels

Prince refused to adhere to gender roles when it came to fashion. He had many styles and fashions that changed during his four decades of being in the public eye. Prince, standing 5' 2", always wore high heels. "People say I'm wearing heels because I'm short. I wear heels because the women like 'em." Prince

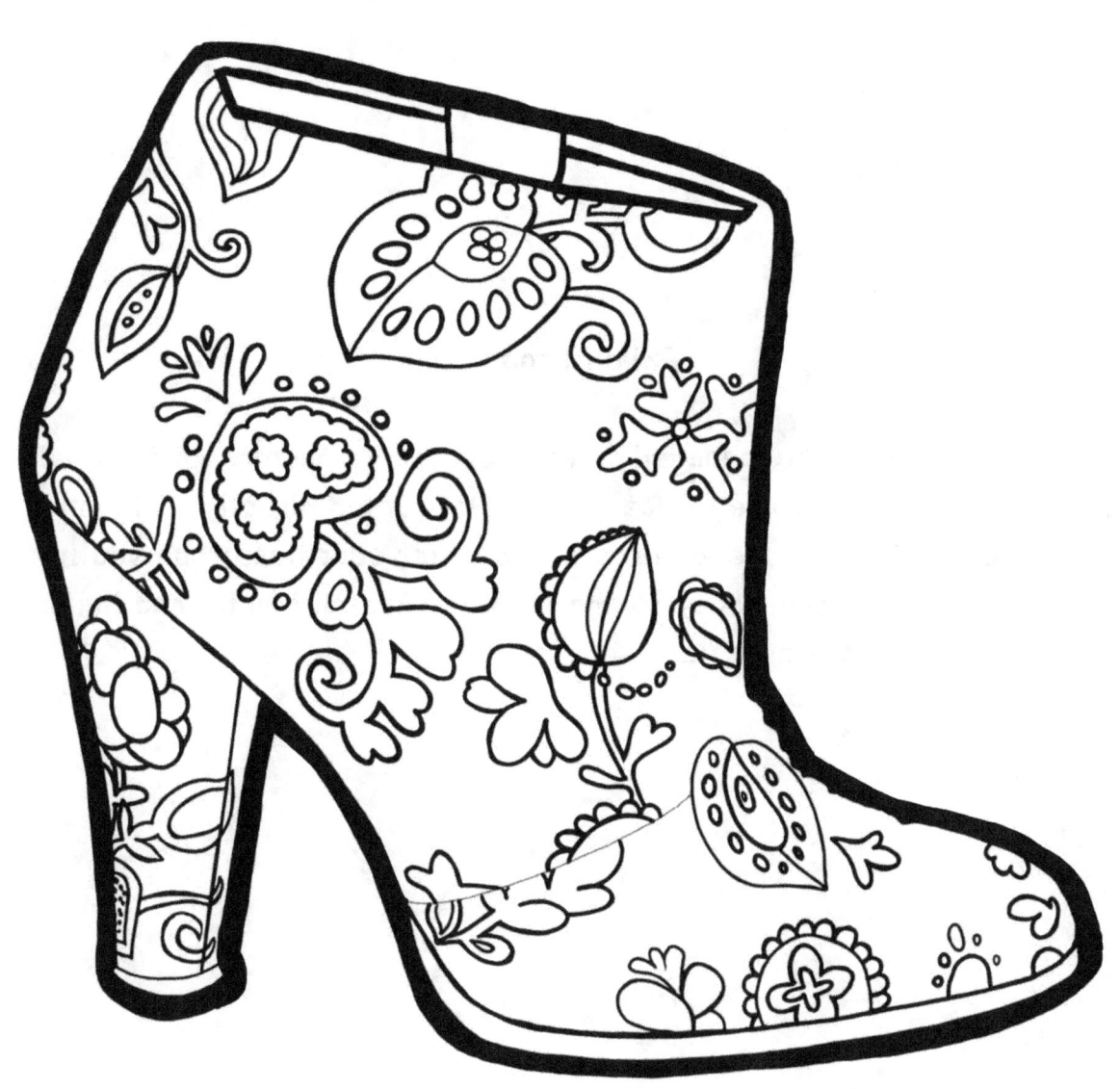

Philanthropist

Prince had another gig he managed to keep secret – philanthropist. We will never know how many people Prince helped. He worked directly with Van Jones to create #YesWeCode, an organization that educates urban youth about technology. He sent money to the family of Travon Martin and helped many music schools in Minnesota.

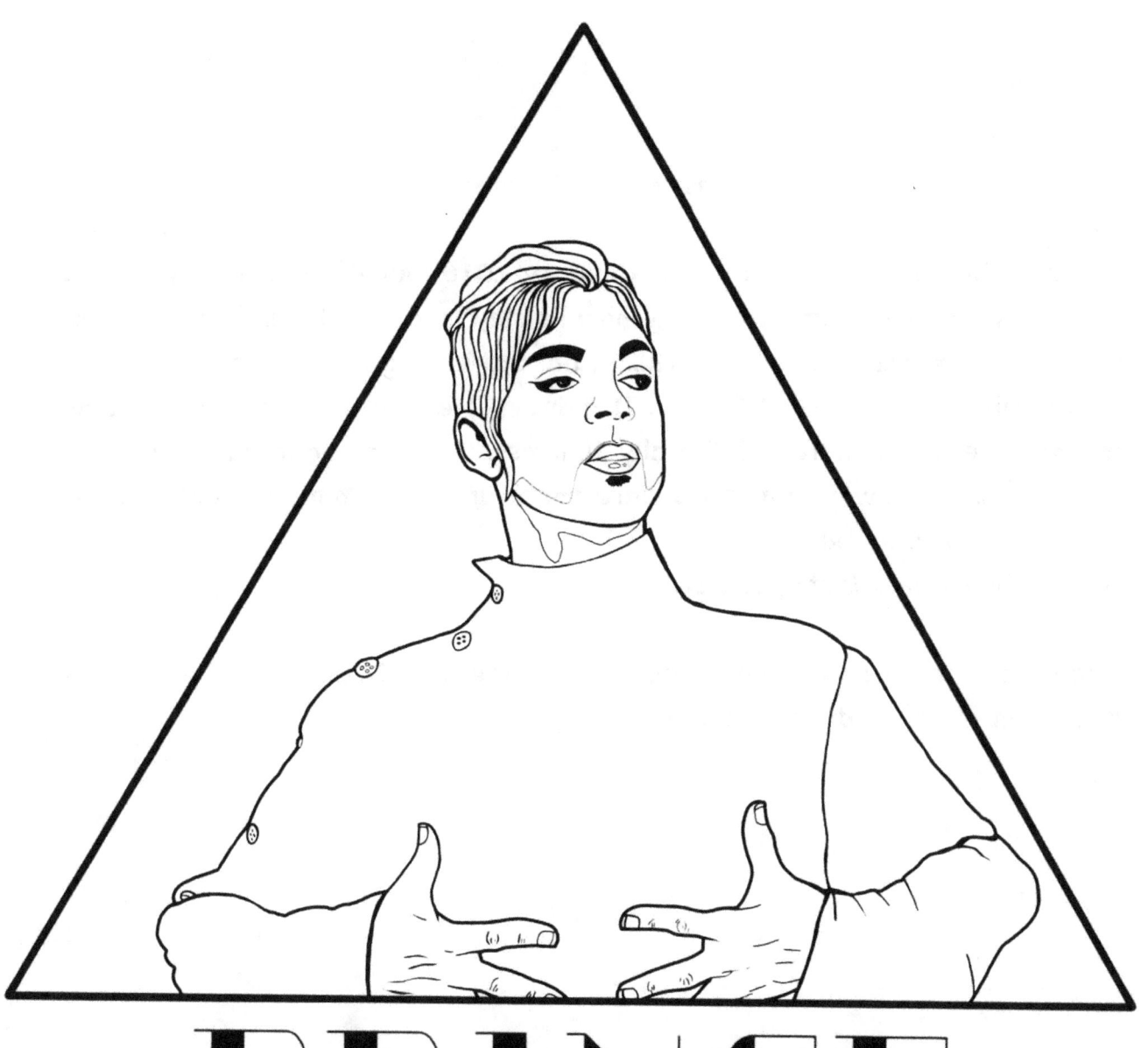

PRINCE

Last Power Generation

"I think the last gig we did was in January 2016, but it's all a blur you know. As far as rehearsal time you know how Paisley is, no clocks and no windows, so time is irrelevant. We just work...ha ha. So, we might go in at 2:00 p.m. and stay until 10:00 p.m. or 11:00 p.m. It didn't matter; no one ever thinks about it when they're in there. It's literally timeless. Once you go in past the foyer, time stops. There were times we were there until 5:00 a.m. and 6:00 a.m. We just didn't care, ha ha."
Adrian Crutchfield Instagram, 2017

(Pictured on next page: Donna Grantis, Dywane MonoNeon Thomas Jr., Prince, Kirk Johnson, and Adrian Crutchfield

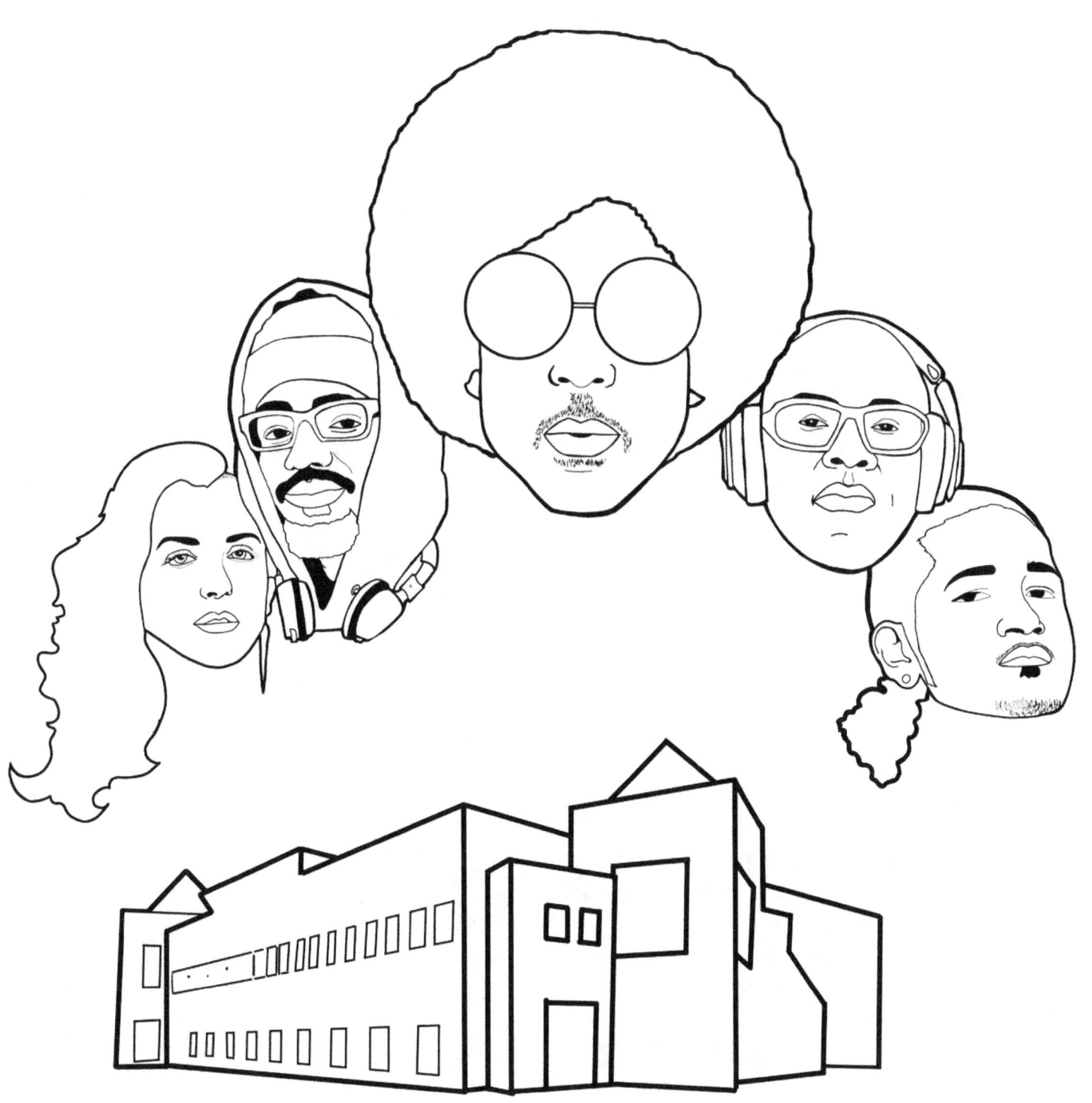